The Chinese Cook Book

The Classic of Oriental Cuisine – Soups, Entrées and Dishes of Meat, Seafood and Game

By Shiu Wong Chan

If you want to keep a man good natured, give him good food.

- E. M. D.

Adansonia Press

Logo art adapted from work by Bernard Gagnon

ISBN-13: 978-0-359-74657-6

First published in 1917

Contents

Preface .... *x*

The History of Chinese Cooking .... *xi*

General Laws of Chinese Cooking .... *xii*

Marketing .... *xiii*

Preliminary Recipes 15

Primary Soup 15

Chinese Sauce 15

Chinese Gravy 16

Sesamum-Seed Oil 16

Peanut Oil 16

Chicken Starch 17

Chinese White Cheese 17

Chinese Red Cheese 17

How to Make Tea 18

Preparation of Secondary Vegetables 18

Soup 18

Bird-Nest Soup 18

Chicken Mushroom Soup 19

Vegetable Soup 19

Duck Soup 20

Pork Soup 20

Fish Soup 21

Noodle Soup 21

Noodle Soup with Chicken and Mushrooms 22

Noodle Soup in Yung Chow Style 22

Noodles 23
    Fried Noodles 23
    Chicken Fried Noodles 23

Chicken 24
    Almond Chicken 24
    Chicken Chop Suey 24
    Chestnut Chicken 25
    Chicken Hash 25
    Chicken Thread 26
    Fried Chicken 26
    Walnut Chicken 26
    Pineapple Chicken 27
    Salt Chicken 27
    Pan Chicken 28
    Bird-Nest in Chicken 28
    Steamed Chicken 29
    Roast Chicken 29

Duck 30
    Roast Duck 30
    Parsley Duck 30
    Duck Hash 31
    Duck Chop Suey 31
    Potato Duck 32
    Wine Vapor Duck 32
    Steamed Duck 33
    East Melon Duck 33
    Fried Duck Feet 34
    Pineapple Duck 35
    Duck Threads 35

- Roast Duck Biscuits 36
- Wild Duck 36
- Ham and Duck 37

Lamb 37
- Fried Lamb 37
- Lamb Hash 37
- Steamed Lamb 38

Chop Suey 38
- Lamb Chop Suey 38
- Plain Chop Suey 39
- Extra Chop Suey 39

Pork 40
- Pork Hash 40
- Pork Threads 40
- Potato Pork 40
- Brittle Pork 41
- Steamed Chestnut Pork 41
- Pork Salad 42
- Fried Pigs' Ribs 42

Beef 43
- Beef Chop Suey 43
- Green Pepper Beef 43

Fish 44
- Fish Chop Suey 44
- Fish Balls 44
- Fried Fish Balls 45
- Raw Fish Party 45
- Fried Fish 46
- Hot Water Fish 46

Steamed Pike 47

Eel 47
Eel in Net 47

Turtle 48
Steamed Turtle 48
Turtle Soup 48

Shark 49
Shark Fins 49

Shrimp 50
Shrimp Chop Suey 50
Steadied Shrimp 50
Fried Shrimp 51

Oysters 51
Oyster Chop Suey 51
Steadied Oysters 52
Roasted Oysters 52

Lobster 53
Lobster Chop Suey 53

Crab 53
Crab Soup 54
Fried Soft-Shell Crab 54

Chinese Tomato 54
Fried Chinese Tomato with Crab 54
Fried Chinese Tomato with Shrimp 55

Pigeon 55
Why Shon Pigeon 55
Pigeon Chop Suey 56
Bird-Nest in Pigeon 56

Fried Pigeon	57
Pigeon Hash	57

Quail 58
Quail Hash	58

Partridge 58
Partridge Hash	58
Partridge Chop Suey	59
Why Shon Partridge	59

Deer 60

Goose 60
Roast Goose	60

Winkle 61

Eggs 61
Plain Omelet	61
Pork Omelet	62
Chicken Omelet	62
Shrimp Omelet	63
Crab Omelet	63
Lobster Omelet	63
Bean Cake Omelet	64
Fried Eggs	64
Egg Roll	65
Checker-Board Eggs	65
Fish Roll	66
Gold and Silver Egg	66
Stuffed Egg	67
Fish Swimming in a Golden Pond	67
Shrimp in Golden Pond	67
Crab in Golden Pond	68

  Lobster in Golden Pond 68

Beans 69

  Bean Sprouts 69

  Bean Cake 69

  Bean Cake Chop Suey 69

  Chicken Starch Bean Cake 70

  Stuffed Triangle Bean Cake 70

  Ruby Mixed with Pearls 71

  Bean Biscuit 71

Stuffed Squash 72

Stuffed Green Peppers 72

Immortal Food 73

  Food of The God of Law Horn 73

  Soft Immortal Food 73

  Hard Immortal Food 74

Dry Foods 74

  Chinese Frankfurter 74

  Chinese Frankfurters on Rice 75

  Chinese Frankfurters with Vegetables 75

  Lamb Frankfurters 76

  Gold and Silver Frankfurters 76

  Spiced Pork 77

  Dry Pork 77

  Spiced Pork with Gray Potatoes 77

  Dry Pork on Rice 78

  Dry Pork with Gray Potatoes 78

  Dried Pork with Fried Bean Cake and Chinese Vegetables 78

  Dry Duck 79

  Dry Duck on Rice 79

    Dry Flat Fish Chop Suey 79

    Dry Flat Fish Soup 80

    Roast Dry Flat Fish 80

Stove Party 81

Rice 81

    Fried Rice 81

Chinese Meat Biscuit 82

Cake 83

    Almond Cake 83

    Chinese Sponge Cake 83

Pudding 84

    Water Chestnut Pudding 84

    Lily-Root Pudding 84

    Gray Potato Pudding 84

Candy 85

    Peanut Candy 85

    Sesamum-Seed Candy 85

Conclusion 86

    The Chemistry of Foods 86

Preface

Someone once said that without a good cook and good cooking life was not worth living.

The author's purpose is to make good cooking possible.

All these recipes have been tested and are therefore reliable.

A person who has tasted Chinese food realizes that it is the most palatable and delicious cooking he ever ate. It is not only that but its nutritious value recommends it to all. It is true in a sense that we eat to live. If the body does not have nutritious and pleasant food no full growth and development is possible; hence power is weakened.

Leave the decision as to Chinese cooking to your own taste. When you have eaten the food you will soon be convinced not only of its merits but, in fact, of its superiority over other kinds of food and ways of cooking.

This book is meant not only for the housewife but also for the restaurateur. In fact, it is written in such a clear, simple form that any one by following its rules can prepare dishes of rare delicacy and flavor.

This is my purpose in writing the book. I wish to make good, tempting, and wholesome cooking possible for all.

Shiu Wong Chan.
New York, May 18, 1917.

Dry Flat Fish Chop Suey	79
Dry Flat Fish Soup	80
Roast Dry Flat Fish	80

Stove Party 81
Rice 81
Fried Rice	81

Chinese Meat Biscuit 82
Cake 83
Almond Cake	83
Chinese Sponge Cake	83

Pudding 84
Water Chestnut Pudding	84
Lily-Root Pudding	84
Gray Potato Pudding	84

Candy 85
Peanut Candy	85
Sesamum-Seed Candy	85

Conclusion 86
The Chemistry of Foods	86

Preface

Someone once said that without a good cook and good cooking life was not worth living.

The author's purpose is to make good cooking possible.

All these recipes have been tested and are therefore reliable.

A person who has tasted Chinese food realizes that it is the most palatable and delicious cooking he ever ate. It is not only that but its nutritious value recommends it to all. It is true in a sense that we eat to live. If the body does not have nutritious and pleasant food no full growth and development is possible; hence power is weakened.

Leave the decision as to Chinese cooking to your own taste. When you have eaten the food you will soon be convinced not only of its merits but, in fact, of its superiority over other kinds of food and ways of cooking.

This book is meant not only for the housewife but also for the restaurateur. In fact, it is written in such a clear, simple form that any one by following its rules can prepare dishes of rare delicacy and flavor.

This is my purpose in writing the book. I wish to make good, tempting, and wholesome cooking possible for all.

Shiu Wong Chan.
New York, May 18, 1917.

The History of Chinese Cooking

In ancient times stoves were very different from now; hence cooking was crude and less elaborate. The food was broiled over coals or buried in hot ashes. The portable stoves of Pompeii which were dug up during the uncovering of the buried city show how these stoves were made. Others were the oven fireplace, the brick oven, and the Franklin stove invented by Benjamin Franklin. The cook-stoves adapted to wood were very different from the gas and electrical appliances of to-day.

It was but a step for primitive man, from baking in hot ashes, or in a covered kettle set on coals, to a simple form of oven. Often one served a community. Sometimes a fire was built directly in the oven, and when it was burned down the oven was swept out and the food put in to be cooked by the heated bricks. The later brick oven, still used in some old houses, had a space underneath for a separate fire. Charcoal was the primitive form of fuel used in some countries, especially in those having a mild climate.

This difference between the stoves of long ago and now has helped to improve our cooking.

The Chinese method of cooking was invented by the Emperor of Pow Hay Se in the year 3000 B.C. Confucius, the great philosopher, taught how to eat scientifically. The proportion of meat should not be more than that of vegetable. There ought to be a little ginger in one's food. Confucius would not eat anything which was not chopped up properly. To-day, unconsciously, the Chinese people are obeying this same law.

It is this scientific custom which makes Chinese food particularly nourishing and beneficial.

In ancient days the Chinese used knives and forks. Later, they found that sometimes these impaired the delicious flavor of the food; hence their use of chop-sticks and spoons.

China has always been noted for its cooking. Many Americans prefer Chinese cooking. In fact, many Americans have Chinese cooks in their kitchens. After having tasted Chinese food, one realizes how delicious it is. It has been said that if the Chinese were as great in other ways as in cooking ability they would notably influence other nations.

The story is told of a young Chinese couple newly married. The bridegroom was boasting to a friend of his bride's ability in cooking. The friend was invited to visit the groom's home. The friend had a keen sense of humor and so he asked the groom if his bride would cook anything he brought. The groom, feeling confident of his wife's ability, told his friend that he might bring anything he wished and the bride would cook it.

The friend came, bringing with him a stalk of sugar-cane and a pound of pork. He gave it to the bride. Now, the friend of course thought it would be impossible for the bride to do anything with these things. But he had not taken into consideration her cleverness.

The bride took the cane and, with a scraper, removed the outside rind. Then she put the pound of pork, cut into pieces, and the remaining cane through a grinder. To this chopped cane she added the white of an egg, and, using a little corn-starch, mixed all well together.

Then she made balls. She fried these balls in oil and proudly set them before their guest, who was astonished at their delicious flavor and tastiness.

This story simply shows the magic of Chinese cooking. Often very tasty and wonderful dishes are made out of unexpected and unusual things. The result is not only savory and appetizing; it creates a desire for more.

Even the inexperienced housewife can prepare Chinese dishes of great flavor and delicacy.

General Laws of Chinese Cooking

A Chinese dish consists of three parts: *(a)* meat; *(b)* secondary vegetables, such as Chinese water chestnut, bamboo shoot, celery, Chinese mushroom, and sometimes other vegetables according to the season; *(c)* the garnish on the top of each dish, consisting of Chinese ham, chicken, or roast pork cut up into small dice or into small bars about one inch long, and enough parsley to aid the taste as well as to ornament the dish.

The amount of meat, in accordance with the hygienic law of Confucius, is about one-third that of the secondary vegetables.

The meat should be the same size and shape as the vegetables and must be uniform. It may be cut into dice, into bars, or into fragments; judgment must be used as to this when the size of the vegetable is limited.

There are three methods employed in Chinese cooking; steaming, frying, and boiling.

In steaming always drain off any water or other liquid substance and add just enough primary soup to cover the material. Steam until just soft, for in that state the food has its most delicious taste. Before eating pour off the primary soup, take off all oil on the surface, and put into the steamer again for a few moments. Salt to suit the taste.

In steaming, a hot fire should be used.

In boiling, the fire should be only sufficiently hot to keep the food at the boiling-point.

Frying should be done over a very hot fire, and the food should be turned constantly with a cooking-shovel, so that every particle will receive the same amount of heat.

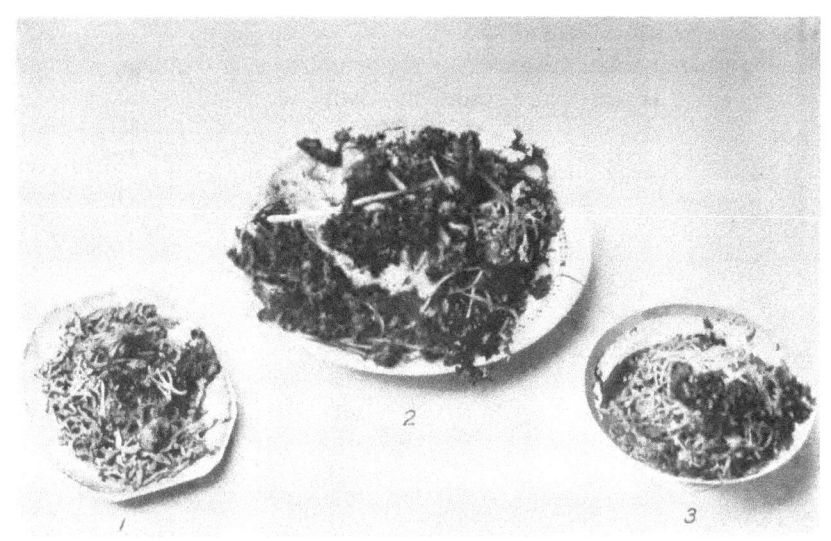

1. Chicken Chow Min
2. Parsley Duck
3. Chicken Chop Suey

Marketing

In addition to the meat and ordinary vegetables, there are articles used in Chinese cooking which are to be found only in Chinese grocery stores. A list of these stores is given in the conclusion.

In ordering by mail, write not only the American or Chinese name of the article, but copy (or trace on thin paper) the Chinese sign for it which will be found, with the approximate cost, in the list.

As the prices can be given only approximately, enclose with your letter a check or money order for 10 per cent, more than the total value of all the articles ordered.

Model Order

March 19, 1917.

Dear Sir:

Enclosed, I send check for $1.00, for which please send me, by express prepaid (or by mail), to the address given below, the following articles:

One bottle of Red Vinegar
10 cents' worth of Octogon Spicery
10 cents' worth of Bug Kay
10 cents' worth of Dong Sum
10 cents' worth of Yen York

Please return by mail the excess of my remittance, and oblige,
Yours very truly,

(Mrs.) John Doe,
25 Marlin Avenue,
New York City.

Preliminary Recipes

Since this is a foreign cook book, it is desirable to have the recipes for all the fundamentals, such as sauces, etc., at the beginning of the book. They not only are nutritious and healthful but are so delicious that they add much to the flavor and delicacy of the foods with which they are combined. As they are used in practically every dish, a thorough knowledge of how to make them is a necessity.

Primary Soup

SUNG TONG

One may wonder why a dish cooked in a restaurant is better than one cooked at home. It is true that a better cook may have some effect on the dish, but the real secret is the primary soup which the cook uses for gravy and for the final cooking instead of using water.

This soup is always made of equal weights of chicken and lean pork: say ½ pound of each, for each pint of water. It is advisable to use not less than 6 pints of water, and meat in proportion.

The quality of a dish depends upon the nature of this primary soup.

(a) Chop the meat into small pieces.

(b) Cook slowly for 2½ hours, or until about half of the liquid has evaporated.

In order to do away with any oil which may exist, put into the mixture a bowl of chicken blood.

(c) Strain through a thick cloth until the liquid is as clear as water. Should there be any oil remaining on top, skim it off.

Let the soup cool. Keep in the refrigerator to be used as needed.

Chinese Sauce

SEE YOUT

Boil Chinese white beans slowly for 6 hours. Strain off the beans and expose the bean soup in a big pot placed under the hot sun. The surface of the liquid turns brown and has a top layer. Remove this layer of brown. A little later take off the other layers, and so on until there is no brown layer. Add salt to this, and boil.

This is called See Yout, meaning sauce. It can be bought, ready prepared, in any Chinese grocery store.

Chinese Gravy

HIN TOUT

1 cup primary soup
1 teaspoonful cornstarch
½ teaspoonful Chinese sauce
Salt, sugar, and a few drops of sesamum-seed oil

Mix the cornstarch well in a little cold water; then stir into the boiling primary soup, and let boil until it thickens. Add the Chinese sauce, salt, sugar, and sesamum-seed oil, and stir well.

Sesamum-Seed Oil

MAR YOUT

Sesamum-seed has the strongest and most delicious oil of any seed. A few drops of this oil will improve a dish greatly.
(a) Roast the seeds in a dry pan with a low fire till they turn brown.
(b) Grind them with a stone grinder, and collect in a pan.
(c) Take off the oil on top. This is sesamum-seed oil.

Peanut Oil

SANG YOUT

Instead of using butter, the Chinese use peanut oil. Therefore in this book the word "oil" means peanut oil unless otherwise stated.
Peanut oil is made as follows:
(a) Skin the peanuts.
(b) Fry them. Turn frequently until they are yellow.
(c) Place them in a hollowed block of thick wood which has a hole in one end. There are smaller holes through which the oil comes when the peanuts are crushed by a stick of wood in the large hole.

Preliminary Recipes

Since this is a foreign cook book, it is desirable to have the recipes for all the fundamentals, such as sauces, etc., at the beginning of the book. They not only are nutritious and healthful but are so delicious that they add much to the flavor and delicacy of the foods with which they are combined. As they are used in practically every dish, a thorough knowledge of how to make them is a necessity.

Primary Soup

SUNG TONG

One may wonder why a dish cooked in a restaurant is better than one cooked at home. It is true that a better cook may have some effect on the dish, but the real secret is the primary soup which the cook uses for gravy and for the final cooking instead of using water.

This soup is always made of equal weights of chicken and lean pork: say ½ pound of each, for each pint of water. It is advisable to use not less than 6 pints of water, and meat in proportion.

The quality of a dish depends upon the nature of this primary soup.

(a) Chop the meat into small pieces.

(b) Cook slowly for 2½ hours, or until about half of the liquid has evaporated.

In order to do away with any oil which may exist, put into the mixture a bowl of chicken blood.

(c) Strain through a thick cloth until the liquid is as clear as water. Should there be any oil remaining on top, skim it off.

Let the soup cool. Keep in the refrigerator to be used as needed.

Chinese Sauce

SEE YOUT

Boil Chinese white beans slowly for 6 hours. Strain off the beans and expose the bean soup in a big pot placed under the hot sun. The surface of the liquid turns brown and has a top layer. Remove this layer of brown. A little later take off the other layers, and so on until there is no brown layer. Add salt to this, and boil.

This is called See Yout, meaning sauce. It can be bought, ready prepared, in any Chinese grocery store.

Chinese Gravy

HIN TOUT

1 cup primary soup
1 teaspoonful cornstarch
½ teaspoonful Chinese sauce
Salt, sugar, and a few drops of sesamum-seed oil

Mix the cornstarch well in a little cold water; then stir into the boiling primary soup, and let boil until it thickens. Add the Chinese sauce, salt, sugar, and sesamum-seed oil, and stir well.

Sesamum-Seed Oil

MAR YOUT

Sesamum-seed has the strongest and most delicious oil of any seed. A few drops of this oil will improve a dish greatly.
(a) Roast the seeds in a dry pan with a low fire till they turn brown.
(b) Grind them with a stone grinder, and collect in a pan.
(c) Take off the oil on top. This is sesamum-seed oil.

Peanut Oil

SANG YOUT

Instead of using butter, the Chinese use peanut oil. Therefore in this book the word "oil" means peanut oil unless otherwise stated.
Peanut oil is made as follows:
(a) Skin the peanuts.
(b) Fry them. Turn frequently until they are yellow.
(c) Place them in a hollowed block of thick wood which has a hole in one end. There are smaller holes through which the oil comes when the peanuts are crushed by a stick of wood in the large hole.

Chicken Starch

GUY YOUNG

2 breasts of chickens
1 cup primary soup
1 teaspoonful cornstarch
White of one egg

(a) Pound the chicken, without skin and bone, as fine as possible. It is best when pounded with a hammer on a chopping-board.

(b) Add the soup, cornstarch, and white of egg. Stir well.

In using chicken starch, never pour it into the substance without first removing the pan from the fire. Keep stirring. Take off the fire the minute it begins to boil. The taste is bad if it boils too long.

Chinese White Cheese

FOO YUE

(a) Cut bean cake, made of Chinese white beans, into half-inch squares ¼ inch thick.

(b) Put into a jar provided with an airtight cover, the size of the jar depending upon the amount to be made.

(c) Fill the jar ¼ full of Fun Wine.

(d) Salt to taste.

(e) Cover air-tight, and put away for not less than two weeks.

Chinese Red Cheese

NOUM YUE

For this the bean cake is made of Chinese red beans.

(a) Wrap up the cakes in a piece of cloth in any desired size. Put pressure on top for 5 days.

(b) Take off the weight. Then the cloth. Scrape off the mold on top.

(c) Place in a jar. Fill the jar ¼ full of Fun Wine, and add plenty of salt.

(d) Cover air-tight, and set away for not less than two weeks; the longer, the better, provided the jar is kept air-tight.

How to Make Tea

Use 1 level teaspoonful of tea to 1 cup of water.

Heat the water until it just reaches the boiling-point, but no more. If you are scientific, insert a thermometer graduated with centigrade degrees. When it reaches 99° remove from the fire at once.

Pour immediately into a half-pint teapot which contains 1 teaspoonful of Chinese tea.

Keep covered for three minutes. Then serve.

Preparation of Secondary Vegetables

Before using any dry substance — such as dry mushrooms, dry chestnuts, etc. — always soak in cool water for ½ hour.

The making of such things as peanut oil, bean cake, Chinese sauce, etc., is practicable only for a factory. Any one without conveniences for making them can readily obtain them from any Chinese grocery store.

The author tells how to make them merely so that you may know what is in them and how they are made. Then you will understand how simple they are, and how healthful and nutritious.

Soup

NOTE: In every recipe given in this book, the quantity stated is sufficient for six persons.

Bird-Nest Soup

YUEN WAR TONG

The substance of which this soup is made is found in bird nests. It is the saliva of the swallows of northern China. It -looks somewhat like spinach. The best quality is pure white. The other quality is a little brown and contains some impurities of straw and feathers, which must be removed by shaking in water.

(a) Soak in cold water for one hour 2 cups of bird-nest. Then wash gently.

(b) Cook in water for 1 hour, with a piece of ginger.

(c) Strain off and put into 6 pints of primary soup. Let simmer for ½ hour.

Serve in bowls or soup-plates, and use 6 teaspoonfuls of Chinese ham and chicken dice for garnish.

For gravy use 3 teaspoonfuls of cornstarch, a few drops of sesamum-seed oil, and salt and pepper to taste.

Chicken Mushroom Soup

MOR GÜE GUY TONG

3 cups Chinese mushrooms, chopped into small dice
¾ cup chicken, chopped to same size
9 cups primary soup
2 eggs
½ teaspoonful cornstarch
1 teaspoonful Chinese sauce
½ teaspoonful oil
Salt, and a few drops of sesamum-seed oil

Chinese mushrooms can be secured at any Chinese grocery store.
(a) Cook the mushrooms for ½ hour, and then drain off and put into the primary soup. Boil for 15 minutes.
(b) Add the chopped chicken; the eggs well beaten; and all the other ingredients. Take off the stove ½ minute after the cornstarch is added.
Serve in bowls. Garnish the top of each bowl with 1 teaspoonful of Chinese ham cut into dice.

Vegetable Soup

CHOY TONG

Any kind of vegetables washed thoroughly and cut into pieces one inch long
Small piece of root ginger
9 cups primary soup
Salt

(a) Heat the cooking pan for ½ minute. Then spread one teaspoonful of oil all over the surface of the pan and let it heat for from 1 to 2 minutes.
(b) Add the salt, then the vegetables and ginger. Turn over frequently until the volume of the vegetables is reduced to 1/3.
(c) Add the primary soup, and let it cook until it boils. Keep the soup boiling slowly until done. The length of time depends upon the kind of vegetables. It is best to keep the pan uncovered.

Duck Soup

ARP TONG

1 medium-sized duck without bones
1 ½ cups Chinese mushrooms
2 cups bamboo shoots
4 cups celery
2 teaspoonfuls oil
A few drops sesamum-seed oil
1 teaspoonful Chinese sauce
¼ teaspoonful cornstarch
Salt

(a) Chop all into dice.
(b) Heat the cooking pan for ½ minute. Then grease it thoroughly with oil.
(c) Add salt and all other ingredients except duck. Keep turning for about 5 minutes.
(d) Add primary soup and boil very slowly.
(e) Mix together well the duck (cut into dice), the oil, sesamum-seed oil, Chinese sauce, and cornstarch.
(f) When primary soup has boiled ½ hour, add the duck mixture. Boil slowly for another ½ hour.
For a garnish, use Chinese ham dice.

Pork Soup

GUE YORK TONG

2 cups lean pork cut into fragments
2 teaspoonfuls cornstarch
2 teaspoonfuls Chinese sauce
5 cups primary soup
2 cups Chinese mushrooms
A few drops sesamum-seed oil
3 cups star melon cut into small pieces after the rind is removed
Salt

(a) Mix the pork, cornstarch, Chinese sauce, and salt.
(b) Bring the primary soup to a boil. Then add the pork mixture and the mushrooms, and cook for ½ hour.
(c) Ten minutes before taking soup off stove, add the melon.

Fish Soup

YUE TONG

1 five-pound fish
5 pints primary soup
2 cups water chestnuts
2 cups bamboo shoots
1 cup Chinese mushrooms

(a) Dress the fish and cook until soft. Take out bones. Tear the meat to pieces (1 ½ inches long).
(b) Cut the secondary vegetables into dice. Cook for 20 minutes.
(c) Put the vegetables and the fish into the primary soup, and cook for 15 minutes.
(d) Add Chinese gravy. Stir the soup well and take from the stove. Serve in bowls. Garnish each bowl.

Noodle Soup

YAT KOI MIN

3 pounds noodles
2 teaspoonfuls Chinese sauce
1 teaspoonful oil
A few drops sesamum-seed oil

Noodles are made of flour, eggs, salt, and a small portion of alkaline solution.

Inasmuch as good noodles require very skilful labor to make them, and they can be obtained much cheaper in a Chinese noodle factory than if made at home, the author does not describe the process.

The best quality contains no water.

To make *yat koi min* (noodle soup) proceed as follows:

(a) Put the noodles into boiling water, and boil until they float on the surface.
(b) Quickly place in cold water and stir.
(c) Put again into boiling water for 1 minute.
(d) Put into a clean bowl containing the oil, sesamum-seed oil, Chinese sauce, and a little pepper.
(e) Divide the noodles into individual portions, and into each bowl pour enough boiling primary soup to cover.

Garnish, and serve hot.

Noodle Soup with Chicken and Mushrooms

MOR GÜE GUY YAT KOI MIN

3 pounds noodles
2 teaspoonfuls Chinese sauce
1 teaspoonful oil
A few drops sesamum-seed oil
1 cup chicken
1 ½ cups mushrooms
1 ½ cups water chestnuts

(a) Put the noodles into boiling water, and boil until they float on the surface.
(b) Quickly place in cold water and stir.
(c) Put again into boiling water for 1 minute.
(d) Put into a clean bowl containing the oil, sesamum-seed oil, Chinese sauce, and a little pepper.
(e) Cut the chicken, mushrooms, and water chestnuts into pieces 1 ½ inches long. Cook until done. Mix together and add Chinese gravy.
(f) Divide the noodles into individual portions, and into each bowl pour enough boiling primary soup to cover.
(g) Add the chicken gravy and serve.

Noodle Soup in Yung Chow Style

YUNG CHOW MIN

Min means noodle, and *Yung Chow* is the name of the place in China where this dish is prepared in the most delicious way.
(a) Put 2 pounds of noodles into boiling water, and boil until the noodles float on the surface.
(b) Take out and place quickly in cold water.
(c) Put into boiling oil until hard.
(d) Cook in 7 cups primary soup until soft.
(e) Make a chicken gravy of 1 cup of chicken fragments, 1 ½ cups Chinese mushrooms, and 1 ½ cups Chinese water chestnuts. Add this to Chinese gravy.
(f) Pour the gravy into the soup, and stir well. Remove from the stove at once, and serve hot.

Noodles

Fried Noodles

CHOW MIN

2 pounds Chinese noodles
1 ½ cups onions cut into threads
1 cup raw pork cut into threads 1 ½ inches long
¾ cup roast pork cut into threads
1 egg fried and cut into threads 1 ½ inches
2 tablespoonfuls lard
1 tablespoonful Chinese sauce
1 tablespoonful cornstarch
3 cups primary soup

Get the noodles from a Chinese noodle store. There are two kinds, so in ordering state that you want noodles for Chow Min.

Egg threads are made by beating an egg well, pouring it into a hot oiled pan, then letting it run all over the surface of the pan, forming a thin layer of yellow egg about one-sixty-fourth inch thick.

To make Chow Min, proceed as follows:

(a) Put the lard on the noodles, and steam for ½ hour.

(b) After the noodles have been steamed, they tend to stay together; therefore it is necessary to loosen them up with a fork.

(c) Place the steamed noodles in a pan of boiling oil and fry until nicely brown. Then put on a dish.

(d) Cook the onion and the pork until done.

(e) Make a gravy of the primary soup, cornstarch (first dissolved in water), Chinese sauce, and salt and pepper. Add the roast pork and egg threads.

(f) Put the onion and pork over the noodles. Pour over this the gravy.

Chicken Fried Noodles

GUY CHOW MIN

1 cup onions cut into threads
2 cupfuls chicken cut into threads 1 ½ inches long
1 egg, fried and cut into threads
1 cup Chinese mushrooms
1 tablespoonful cornstarch
1 tablespoonful Chinese sauce

3 cups primary soup
2 tablespoonfuls lard

(a) Put the lard on the noodles, and steam for ½ hour.
(b) After the noodles have been steamed, they tend to stay together; therefore they should be loosened up with a fork.
(c) Place the steamed noodles in a pan of boiling oil and fry until nicely brown. Then put on a dish.
(d) Cook the onion and chicken until done.
(e) Make a gravy of the primary soup, cornstarch (first dissolved in water), Chinese sauce, and salt and pepper. Add the mushrooms and the egg threads to the gravy.
(f) Put the onion and chicken over the noodles. Pour over this the gravy.

Chicken

Almond Chicken

HUNG YUEN GUY DING

2 cups almonds
2 cups onions cut into dice
2 cups water chestnuts cut into dice
2 cups mushrooms cut into dice
1 cup celery cut into dice
1 pound of chicken, without bones

(a) Skin the almonds by putting in boiling water. Fry in boiling oil until they turn yellow.
(b) Put the water chestnuts, onions, mushrooms, and celery in a hot cooking pan containing some oil, and fry rapidly. Keep them moving, so that each particle receives the same amount of heat. Add water enough to cover and boil for 15 minutes.
(c) Put the chicken in a hot oiled pan and fry for 2 minutes. Add enough primary soup to cover, and cook, with the cover on, for 10 minutes.
(d) Add Chinese gravy. Take from the stove at once.
(e) Put the chicken on a dish and add the secondary vegetables (onions, water chestnuts, etc.). On top of this put the almonds.

Chicken Chop Suey

CHOW GUY PIN

1 chicken cut into fragments
2 cups water chestnuts
2 cups mushrooms
2 cups bamboo shoots
2 cups celery cut into thin pieces

This dish is not known in China. From the name it means simply a variety of small pieces. However, the principles of Chinese cooking are the same.

(a) Put the water chestnuts, mushrooms, bamboo shoots, and celery into a hot pan containing oil. Fry for 2 minutes. Add water and cook for 15 minutes.
(b) Put the chicken in a frying-pan containing oil and fry for 5 minutes.
(c) Add the secondary vegetables and mix well.
(d) Add enough primary soup to cover, and cook for 5 minutes.
(e) Add Chinese gravy and stir. Remove from the stove at once.

Chestnut Chicken

LUT GE GUY

1 cup chicken
2 cups chestnuts
2 cups water chestnuts 2 cups mushrooms

(a) Cut the chicken into pieces ¾ inch by 1½ inches. Cut the chestnuts, water chestnuts, and mushrooms into big pieces.
(b) Rub salt and a little Chinese sauce on the chicken. Then put into a pot of boiling oil until the color becomes yellow.
(c) Now put into primary soup and boil until nearly soft.
(d) Add the secondary vegetables and cook until done.
No gravy is necessary with *Lut Ge Guy.*
Serve hot and add parsley for garnish.

Chicken Hash

GUY SUNG

1 chicken cut into very small pieces
2 cups each of water chestnuts, mushrooms, and bamboo shoots, chopped fine
½ teaspoonful of ginger juice
½ teaspoonful of Fun Wine
1 head of lettuce cut into threads

1 tablespoonful of Chinese ham cut into dice
1 handful of fried noodles

(a) Fry the chopped chicken in a hot, oiled pan.
(b) Add the ginger juice and Fun Wine. Then the chopped water chestnuts, mushrooms, and bamboo shoots. Mix well.
(c) Add enough primary soup to cover and cook until done.
(d) Add Chinese gravy and remove from the stove at once.
(e) Salt to suit the taste.
Serve on top of lettuce. Use the Chinese ham dice and the fried noodles as a garnish.

Chicken Thread

GUY SUE

1 chicken cut into threads
2 cups bamboo shoots
2 cups Chinese mushrooms

(a) Cook the bamboo shoots and mushrooms for 20 minutes. Then mix with the chicken.
(b) Add enough primary soup to cover and cook for 5 minutes.
(c) Add Chinese gravy and remove from the stove at once.

Fried Chicken

GAR GEE GUY

(a) Put 3 spring chickens, of about 2 pounds each, into a jar of Chinese sauce for 10 minutes.
(b) Place in a pan of boiling oil and fry until the chickens turn yellow.
(c) Cut up and serve hot.
Use spicery salt on top of the chicken. To make spicery salt, fry together for 15 minutes an equal amount of spicery powder and salt. Have a low fire and turn frequently to prevent burning.

Walnut Chicken

HOP TOO GUY DING

3 cups English walnuts

2 cups onions cut into dice
2 cups water chestnuts cut into (dice
1½ cups celery cut into dice
1 pound of chicken without bones

(a) Remove the skins from the walnuts by placing them in boiling water. Then fry them in boiling oil until they turn yellow.
(b) Put the secondary vegetables in a hot cooking-pan containing oil and fry for 2 or 3 minutes. Keep them moving so that each particle receives the same amount of heat. Add enough primary soup to cover and boil for 15 minutes.
(c) Put the chicken in a hot, oiled pan and fry for 2 minutes.
(d) Add the vegetables.
(e) Add Chinese gravy and remove from the stove.
Place on a dish and garnish with the fried walnuts.

Pineapple Chicken

BOR LOR GUY

1 chicken
1 can pineapple
2 cups green peppers 2 cups celery
1 cup canned sour ginger ½ cup vinegar
½ cup Fun Wine
2 eggs

(a) Cut the chicken, pineapple, peppers, celery, and ginger into pieces 1½ inches long.
(b) Break the eggs into the chicken and mix well together with a little cornstarch and salt. Then put into boiling oil and fry until all becomes yellow.
(c) Put the pineapple, pepper, celery, and ginger into a hot, oiled pan and fry for 2 minutes. Add the fried chicken. Mix well and add the Fun Wine. Cook over a hot fire for 5 minutes; then add enough primary soup to cover and cook until about one cup of liquid is left.
(d) Add the vinegar and a little sugar.
(e) Pour Chinese gravy over the chicken. Mix well together, and serve at once.

Salt Chicken

YIM GUY

1 whole chicken dried well inside and out

Rock salt enough to cover the chicken
¼ cup of spicery salt

(a) Put the salt into a hot pan and leave over the fire until the salt gets very hot.
(b) In a suitable pan bury the chicken in this hot salt, covering the chicken entirely. Cover the pan and keep air-tight for 2 hours.
(c) Take out the chicken and shake off all salt.
(d) Cut up the chicken and sprinkle the spicery salt over it. Chicken prepared in this way tastes delicious, and is not salty.

Pan Chicken

WATT GUY

1 cup lily flower
1 cup fungus
2 cups dry mushrooms
1 chicken
A small piece of ginger root, without the skin
¼ cup of Fun Wine

(a) Soak the lily flower, fungus, and the mushrooms in cold water for ½ hour.
(b) Wash the chicken inside and outside with Chinese sauce. Put in a pan with oil and fry for 10 minutes. Add the Fun Wine and salt. Add 2 cups of water.
(c) Now put all into a small pot and add the lily flower, fungus, mushrooms, and ginger. Keep cover on tight and cook for ½ hour over a slow fire.
This is the most delicious chicken ever known.

Bird-Nest in Chicken

FONG TUNG YUEN

1½ cups bird-nest
1 large whole chicken (at least 7 pounds)
1 bowl primary soup
1 tablespoonful Chinese ham

(a) Soak the bird-nest in cold water for 1 hour. Then wash gently and cook for 1 hour with a piece of ginger.

(b) Pick the chicken, chop off the head, feet and wings, cut 1 line 4 inches long and take out the interior. Clean the chicken and rub inside and outside with salt. Place in a bowl with the cut side on top.

(c) Fill the chicken with the bird-nest and the primary soup. Steam for 3 hours in a double-boiler.

(d) Now transfer into a second bowl by using a bowl a little larger than the first bowl and putting this second bowl on top of the first bowl mouth to mouth.

Garnish with the Chinese ham dice.

Steamed Chicken

GING GUY

1 chicken cut into pieces about 1½ inches long
2 cups mushrooms
A few slices of ginger root
4 pieces of red dates
1 Chinese onion
Cornstarch, sauce, salt, and oil

(a) Mix well the chicken, oil, salt, cornstarch, and sauce.

(b) Add mushrooms, ginger root, and red dates. Put on a plate and steam for ½ hour.

(c) Add Chinese onion cut into threads 1½ inches long.

Garnish with parsley. Serve with mustard, sauce, and oil.

Roast Chicken

SUE GUY

2 chickens (about 4 pounds each)
2 teaspoonfuls spicery powder
2 cups Chinese sauce
A few drops of sesamum-seed oil
2 teaspoonfuls salt

(a) Put the chickens in hot, not boiling, water for 2 minutes and then add the spicery powder, sauce, oil, and salt. Leave the chickens in for 20 minutes. Be sure every bit of chicken is dipped into it.

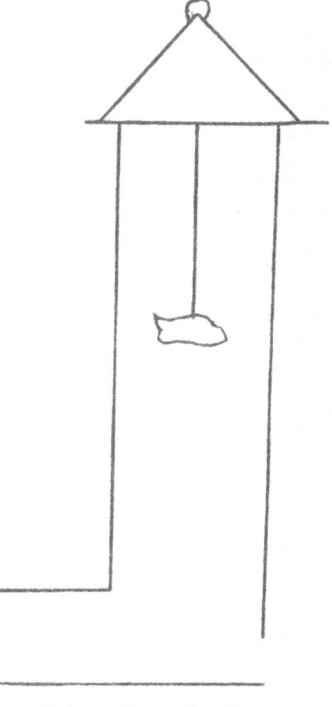

Chinese Roasting Stove

(b) Place the chickens as shown in the diagram, having first started the fire, that the wall is hot. Roast for 1 hour.

A hot fire is necessary before the chickens are put into the stove; after the chickens are in, the fire must be kept low. There must be no smoke.

Duck

Roast Duck

SUE ARP

2 ducks (about 4 pounds each)
2 teaspoonfuls spicery powder
2 cups Chinese sauce
A few drops of sesamum-seed oil
2 teaspoonfuls salt

(a) Put the ducks in hot, not boiling, water for 2 minutes and then add the spicery powder, sauce, oil, and salt. Leave the ducks in for 20 minutes. Be sure every bit of duck is dipped into it.

(b) Place the ducks as shown in the diagram, having first started the fire, that the wall is hot. Roast for 1 hour.

A hot fire is necessary before the ducks are put into the stove; after the ducks are in, the first must be kept low. There must be no smoke.

Parsley Duck

SI WO ARP

2 ducks
2 cups mushrooms
2 small pieces ginger root, mashed
1 tablespoonful Fun Wine
Parsley enough to cover the dish 1 inch thick

(a) Open the ducks with one 4-inch cut in the back of each. Take out the interior. Wash thoroughly and dry. Now wash the ducks inside and out with sweet sauce.

(b) Cook the duck in a pan of boiling oil until yellow.

(c) Put the duck into a frying-pan. Cover with the mushrooms, ginger, and Fun Wine. Add 1/3 more than enough primary soup to cover all. Cook until the duck is done.

When done, there must be 3 cups of liquid left. Therefore, the amount of primary soup used depends on the age and size of the duck, because the older the duck the longer it takes to cook.

(d) Make a gravy of the liquid left, with cornstarch, sauce, sesamum-seed oil, and salt.

(e) Place the duck on top of the parsley. Pour the gravy over all, and garnish with Chinese ham.

Duck Hash

ARP SUNG

1 duck chopped into pieces as small as possible
2 cups water chestnuts chopped fine
2 cups mushrooms chopped fine
½ teaspoonful ginger juice
½ teaspoonful Fun Wine
1 head of lettuce cut into threads
2 cups fried noodles

(a) Fry the chopped duck in a hot, oiled pan. Add the ginger juice and Fun Wine. Then add the chopped water chestnuts, mushrooms, and bamboo shoots. Mix well. Add enough primary soup to cover and cook until done.

(b) Add Chinese gravy, and salt to suit the taste. Serve on top of lettuce. Use the Chinese ham dice and the fried noodles as a garnish.

Duck Chop Suey

CHOW ARP PIN

1 chicken
2 cups water chestnuts
2 cups mushrooms
2 cups bamboo shoots
2 cups celery
2 cups primary soup

(a) Cut the chicken and all of the vegetables into small pieces.

(b) Put the secondary vegetables into a hot pan containing oil. Fry for 2 minutes. Add water and cook for 15 minutes.

(c) Place the duck fragments in a hot, oiled pan and fry for 5 minutes.

(d) Add the secondary vegetables and mix well.

(e) Add the primary soup and cook for 5 more minutes.

(f) Add Chinese gravy. Mix well and serve at once.

Potato Duck

SU JAI ARP

1 duck (about 7 pounds)
The same amount of skinned potatoes
A cake of Chinese red cheese
1 small piece of ginger, pounded
¼ cup Fun Wine
A piece of green carrot

(a) Put the duck into an oiled frying-pan and fry until brown. Turn frequently, so that every part of the duck receives the same amount of heat.

(b) Add the ginger and Fun Wine and fry for 2 minutes. Take out and put into a bowl. The liquid left in the frying-pan is to be put into a separate bowl.

(c) Add 2 cups of water to the cheese and mash. Rub this well into the duck, inside and outside.

(d) Put the potatoes into the cooking-pan. Place the duck on top. Add enough water to cover all. Over this pour any cheese liquid which remains. Add the carrot.

(e) Cover the pan and cook until tender.

Wine Vapor Duck

SUN SIN ARP

2 ducks (about 4 pounds each)
2 cups, ¾ full, of any wine
1 teaspoonful spicery salt
2 tablespoonfuls Chinese ham

(a) Open the ducks with one cut about 4 inches long in the back of each.

(b) When the ducks have been cleaned, place them in a suitable bowl with the back upward.

(c) Rub the duck inside and out with spicery salt.

(d) Place carefully in each duck one of the cups of wine. Be sure the wine does not spill on the duck.

(e) Steam in a double-boiler for 2½ hours, or until tender.

(f) Remove cover. Pour in cold water to stop the steam. By means of a cloth take out the cups of wine.

(g) Pour off the gravy into another bowl. Skim off the oil.

(h) Place over the bowl containing the duck a second bowl a little larger than the first. Turn the first bowl upside down so that the duck falls into the second bowl.

(i) Now pour the gravy back over the duck.

Garnish with the Chinese ham cut into small oblong pieces and with a little parsley.

Steamed Duck

DON JUN AEP

1 duck (about 8 pounds)
2 cups chestnuts without skins
1 cup barley
½ cup white nuts without skins
1 tablespoonful Fun Wine

(a) Soak the chestnuts and barley in cold water for 1 hour.

(b) Open the back of the duck with one cut about 4 inches long. Take out the bones without tearing the meat.

(c) When the duck has been cleaned wash it inside and out with Chinese sauce. Salt thoroughly and put into a hot, oiled pan and fry for 10 minutes.

(d) Add the Fun Wine. Turn the duck frequently.

(e) Now put the duck, with the open side upward, in a bowl a little larger than the duck. Fill with the chestnuts, barley, and white nuts and any juice left in the frying-pan.

(f) Steam for 2½ hours.

(g) Pour off the gravy into another bowl. Skim off the oil.

(h) Transfer the duck carefully into a larger bowl by holding the bowls mouth to mouth.

(i) Pour the gravy over the duck and serve.

East Melon Duck

DUNG QUAR ARP

1 boneless duck cut into small dice
1 east melon (8 inches in diameter)
1 handful skinned water chestnuts cut into small dice
1 handful lotus nuts
1 handful mushrooms cut into small dice
1 small piece of ginger without the skin, pounded
1 teaspoonful Fun Wine

(a) Cut off the top of the melon as shown in the picture. Take out the seeds.

(b) Oil the cooking-pan and heat.

(c) Fry the duck for 10 minutes.

(d) Add the ginger and Fun Wine. Salt. Fry for 1 minute more. Turn frequently.

(e) Add chestnuts, lotus nuts, mushrooms, and enough primary soup to fill the melon. Cook until the soup boils.

(f) Transfer all into the melon. Cover with the piece you cut from the melon. Steam for about 3½ hours; the size of melon decides the length of time necessary for steaming.

(g) Remove from the stove. Add cold water to stop the steam. Take the melon out of the pan. Take off the cover of the melon. By means of a spoon take off any oil which has formed on the top.

(h) Scoop out the melon and mix well with the duck and other ingredients. Be careful not to break the rind.

Serve hot.

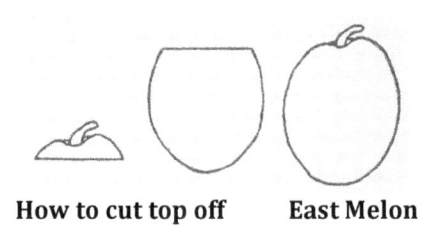

How to cut top off   **East Melon**

Fried Duck Feet

CHOW ARP GUNG

You may laugh all you want. You will soon be convinced that this is the best part of the duck after you taste it.

20 pairs of duck feet
2 cups chopped bamboo shoots
2 cups mushrooms. Cut the larger ones
2 cups water chestnuts cut into thin pieces

(a) Wash thoroughly 20 pairs of duck feet and plunge them into boiling water for 3 minutes. Take off the skin. Take out all bones without spoiling the shape of the feet. Cut each foot into 2 pieces.

(b) Cut into small pieces the bamboo shoots, mushrooms, and water chestnuts.

(c) Have a hot stove. Oil the frying-pan and fry the feet for 5 minutes. Add salt and the bamboo shoots, chestnuts and mushrooms. Continue to fry for 5 minutes after having mixed well.

(d) Add enough primary soup or water to cover all. Cook until tender.

(e) Add Chinese gravy and mix well.

Pineapple Duck

BOR LOB ARP

1 duck
1 can of pineapple
2 cups green peppers
2 cups celery
4 pieces of canned sour ginger
¼ cup Fun Wine
2 eggs

(a) Cut into small oblong pieces the duck, pineapple, peppers, celery, and ginger.
(b) Break the eggs into the duck and mix well together with a little cornstarch and salt.
(c) Put the pineapple, pepper, celery, and ginger into a hot, oiled pan and fry for 2 minutes.
(d) Add the fried duck. Mix well and add the Fun Wine. Have a hot fire. After 5 minutes add enough primary soup to cover the substances and cook until about one cup of liquid is left.
(e) Add the vinegar and sugar and mix with Chinese gravy.

Duck Threads

ARP SUE

1 duck
2 cups bamboo shoots
2 cups mushrooms
3 cups primary soup

(a) Cook the duck until tender and tear off the meat into shreds.
(b) Cook the bamboo shoots and mushrooms for 20 minutes. Then mix with the duck.
(c) Add the primary soup and cook a while longer.
(d) Add Chinese gravy, mix well, and serve.

Roast Duck Biscuits

SUE ARP BOW

1 duck
2 pounds flour
½ cup lard
1 tablespoonful salt
4 tablespoonfuls baking powder

(a) Roast the duck, take out the bones, and cut the meat into small pieces.

(b) Sift the flour and put into a suitable bowl. Mix the flour with enough cold water to make a thin dough.

(c) Roll the dough out flat and cut into the size of biscuits.

(d) Now roll the biscuits flat and fill them with the duck meat, wrapping the dough around the meat into a perfect ball. Close it up carefully. The amount of duck should be one-half the amount of dough.

(e) Place in a double-boiler for 10 minutes before putting over the fire. Steam for ¾ of an hour.

Wild Duck

YAR ARP

1 duck
2 cups chestnuts without skins
2 cups water chestnuts
1 cup chopped pork
1 cup barley
½ cup white nuts without skins

(a) Soak the chestnuts and the barley in cold water for 1 hour.

(b) Open the back of the duck with one cut about 4 inches long. Take out the bones without tearing the meat.

(c) Wash the duck inside and out with Chinese sauce. Salt thoroughly and put into an oiled pan and fry for 10 minutes. Add the Fun Wine. Turn the duck frequently. Take from the stove and put into a bowl a little larger than the duck.

(d) Fill the duck with the chestnuts, barley, nuts and any juice left in the frying-pan. Steam for 2½ hours.

(e) Get a bowl larger than the one holding the duck and place that on top of the other one, mouth to mouth. Use a cloth to protect the hand from getting burned. Carefully pour the gravy off into a third bowl and take off any oil. Turn the duck upside down so it will fall into the new bowl.

(f) Pour the gravy over the duck and serve.

Ham and Duck

FOR TOY ARP

(a) Take the bones out of 1 duck. Then boil the duck for 15 minutes.

(b) Boil Chinese ham for 15 minutes and then cut into pieces 1/16 inch by ¾ inch by 1½ inches. There should be 1/3 as much ham as duck.

(c) Put in a bowl 1 piece of duck, 1 piece of ham, and so on, until the bowl is filled.

(d) Add 2 cups primary soup and 1 cup Fun Wine, and steam for 2½ hours.

Lamb

Fried Lamb

HONG SUE MIN YUNG

3 pounds of lamb cut into pieces ½ inch by 1½ inches by 6 inches
A few drops of Octogon spicery
1 bunch garlic
1 teaspoonful salt

(a) Put the lamb, spicery, garlic, and salt into a pan of cold water, more than enough to cover the substances, and cook until tender.

(b) Take out the lamb and throw away the rest of the substance. Dip the lamb into a dish of salt and Chinese sauce.

(c) Fry the lamb in a pan of boiling oil until brittle.

(d) Chop up fried lamb into proper size and serve when hot. Use spicery salt to suit the taste.

Lamb Hash

MIN YUNG SUNG

2 pounds of lamb
2 cups water chestnuts
2 cups mushrooms
2 cups bamboo shoots
1 head lettuce cut into threads
2 tablespoonfuls Chinese ham cut into dice
1 cup fried noodles
1 tablespoonful Fun Wine
½ teaspoonful ginger juice

The lamb, water chestnuts, mushrooms, and bamboo shoots are to be chopped as fine as possible.

(a) Fry the chopped lamb in a hot, oiled pan.

(b) Add the ginger juice and Fun Wine. Then add the chopped water chestnuts, mushrooms, and bamboo shoots. Mix well.

(c) Add enough primary soup to cover and cook until done. Serve on top of the lettuce threads.

Steamed Lamb

DON MIN YUNG

2 pounds of lamb cut into pieces ¾ inch by 1½ inches by ¾ inch
2 cups dry mushrooms
2 cups unskinned chestnuts
3 red dates
1 cup Fun Wine

(a) Use water to boil the lamb for 10 minutes.

(b) Take out the lamb and dip into a bowl of salt and sweet sauce (Chinese name *Chew Yout*).

(c) Put all into a suitable bowl. Add enough primary soup to cover and add the chestnuts, red dates, and Fun Wine. Steam until tender.

(d) Remove any oil from the liquid, and serve.

Chop Suey

Lamb Chop Suey

CHOW MIN YUNG

1½ pounds lamb
25 threads skinless ginger root
2 cups bamboo shoots
2 cups dry mushrooms
1 cup fried noodles

(a) Cut all the ingredients except the noodles into threads 1½ inches long.

(b) Fry the ginger root, bamboo shoots, and mushrooms in a hot, oiled pan for 10 minutes.

(c) Add the lamb. Mix well. Cook for 5 more minutes.

(d) Add one bowl of primary soup and cook until 1 cup of liquid is left.
(e) Add Chinese gravy.
Use the fried noodles for a garnish. Serve when hot.

Plain Chop Suey

EARN CHOP

2 pounds pork
2 pounds bean sprouts
2 cups onion threads

(a) Cut the pork into pieces 1/16 inch by ½ inch by 1 inch.
(b) Put the pork, bean sprouts, and onions into an oiled pan and fry for 10 minutes.
(c) Add water enough to cover and cook for 15 minutes.
(d) Add Chinese gravy.

Extra Chop Suey

GAR LEW CHOP

2 pounds pork cut into pieces 1/16 inch by ½ inch by 1 inch
Bean sprouts equal to amount of pork
2 cups onions cut into threads
2 cups bamboo shoots cut into pieces same size as pork
2 cups mushrooms

(a) Put the pork, bean sprouts, onions, bamboo shoots and mushrooms into an oiled pan and fry for 10 minutes.
(b) Add water enough to cover and cook for 15 minutes.
(c) Add Chinese gravy.
Remove from the stove and serve at once.

Pork

Pork Hash

GE YORK SUNG

1½ pounds pork
2 cups water chestnuts
2 cups mushrooms
2 cups bamboo shoots
½ teaspoonful ginger juice

1 teaspoonful Fun Wine
1 head lettuce cut into threads
2 tablespoonfuls Chinese ham cut into dice
1 cup fried noodles

The pork, water chestnuts, mushrooms, and bamboo shoots are to be chopped as fine as possible.
 (a) Fry the chopped pork in a hot, oiled pan.
 (b) Add the ginger juice and Fun Wine. Then add the chopped water chestnuts, mushrooms, and bamboo shoots. Mix well,
 (e) Add enough primary soup to cover and cook until done. Serve on top of the lettuce threads.

Pork Threads

GE YORK SE

1½ pounds pork
2 cups bamboo shoots
2 cups mushrooms
3 cups primary soup

 (a) Cook the pork until tender and tear off the meat into threads.
 (b) Cook the bamboo shoots and mushrooms for 20 minutes. Then mix with the pork.
 (c) Add the primary soup and cook again.
 (d) Add Chinese gravy.

Potato Pork

SE JI GE YORK

Pork (2 pounds)
4 pounds skinned potatoes
1 small piece ginger, pounded

1 cake Chinese red cheese
½ cup Fun Wine
1 piece green carrot

(a) Oil the frying-pan. Put in the pork. Fry until brown. Turn frequently so that every part of the pork receives the same amount of heat.
(b) Add the ginger and the wine and fry for 2 minutes.
(c) Take out and put into a bowl. Put the juice left in the frying-pan into a separate bowl.
(d) Add 2 cups of water to the red cheese and mash.
(e) Put the potatoes into a cooking-pan. Add the carrot. Place the pork on top. Add enough water to cover. Pour over this the juice and the cheese.
(f) Cover the pan and cook for 1½ hours.

Brittle Pork

SO JOU GE YORK

3 pounds pork cut into pieces ¾ inch by 1½ inches by ¼ inch
A few pieces of Octogon spicery
2 tablespoonfuls Fun Wine
1 egg
1 tablespoonful cornstarch

(a) Boil the pork and spicery in plain water for 10 minutes. Let cool.
(b) Break the egg. Mix with the cornstarch. Then mix with the pork.
(c) Fry in boiling oil until it gets red.
(d) Put the fried pork into cold water and change water several times until no oil floats on the surface.
(e) Dry the pork and place in a bowl.
(f) Add the Fun Wine, and steam for 2 hours.

Steamed Chestnut Pork

LUT GE DONG GE YORK

2½ pounds pork cut into pieces 1 inch by ¾ inch by 1½ inches
2 cups skinless chestnuts
1 cup Fun Wine

(a) Dip the pork into sweet sauce and fry in boiling oil until red.
(b) Take out the pork and place in cold water. Change water until no oil is on top of the water.

(c) Dry fried pork and place in a bowl.
(d) Add the chestnuts and the Fun Wine.
Steam for 1¾ hours.

Pork Salad

LANG BONG GE YORK

2½ pounds pork (uncut)
2½ pounds string beans cut 2 inches long
½ cup mustard
1 cup vinegar

(a) Boil the pork until done and place in cold water. Punch several small holes with a large needle. Gently squeeze the oil out of it. Change water until no oil is on the top.
(b) Cut the pork into thin pieces 1/32 inch by ½ inch by 1½ inches. Mix with salt to suit the taste, and with the mustard and vinegar.
(c) Boil the string beans for 10 minutes. Put into a bowl, and add salt and enough vinegar to cover.
(d) Cover and keep air tight for 2 hours.
(e) Place the pork on top of the string beans and serve.
Use parsley and sage cut into threads for a garnish.

Fried Pigs' Ribs

CHOW PAI QUIT

4 pounds pigs' ribs
1 cup vinegar
2 teaspoonfuls sugar
1 cup Fun Wine
2 teaspoonfuls cornstarch
1 teaspoonful Chinese sauce
1 egg

(a) Cut the ribs into pieces ¾ inch by ¾ inch by 1½ inches, and mix well with the egg, Chinese sauce, salt, 1 teaspoonful cornstarch and 1 teaspoonful sugar. Fry in boiling oil until brown.
(b) Add to the mixture the vinegar. Fun Wine, 2 cups of water, and the remaining sugar and cornstarch. Cook until nearly dry.

Beef

Beef Chop Suey

CHOW OUT YORK PIN

½ pound beef
4 cups celery cut into pieces ½ inch long
2 cups bean sprouts
½ teaspoonful cornstarch
½ teaspoonful Fun Wine
A few pieces sesamum-seed oil
A few threads ginger root

(a) Cut the beef into pieces 1/32 inch by ½ inch by 1½ inches. Mix thoroughly with the cornstarch, sesamum-seed oil, Fun Wine, and a little salt and Chinese sauce.

(b) Put the celery and bean sprouts into a hot, oiled pan and fry for 5 minutes.

(c) Add water enough to cover. Spread the beef on top. Cover tightly and cook until nearly dry.

(d) Add Chinese gravy and mix well.

Green Pepper Beef

LAR GUE OUT

2 pounds beef
2 cups green peppers cut into pieces 1 inch by 1 inch
1 cup celery, chopped
1 cup bean sprouts
½ teaspoonful cornstarch
½ teaspoonful Fun Wine
A few pieces sesamum-seed oil
A few threads ginger root

(a) Cut the beef into pieces 1/32 inch by ¾ inch by 1½ inches. Mix with the cornstarch oil, sesamum-seed oil, and Chinese sauce.

(b) Put the celery, bean sprouts, and green peppers into a hot, oiled pan and fry for 5 minutes.

(c) Add water enough to cover. Spread the beef on top. Cover tightly and cook until nearly dry.

(d) Add Chinese gravy and mix well.

Fish

Fish Chop Suey

CHOW YUE PIN

5 pounds pike not less than 2½ inches in diameter. Take out bones and cut into thin fragments
2 cups mushrooms
A few pieces of ginger cut into pieces 1/32 inch by ¾ inch by 1 inch
2 cups bamboo shoots cut into pieces ¾ by 1½ inches by 1/32 inch.
2 cups bean sprouts

(a) Remove the skin from the pike and take out the bones. Cut into pieces 1/16 inch thick.
(b) Fry the mushrooms, ginger, bamboo shoots, and bean sprouts in a hot, oiled pan for 5 minutes.
(c) Add water enough to cover all. Cook for 15 minutes.
(d) Add Chinese gravy.
(e) Add the pike and mix well. Garnish with parsley, and serve hot.

Fish Balls

YUE YUN

6 pounds pike
1½ cups salted almonds or peanuts
½ cup Chinese ham
6 pounds vegetables in season
1 teaspoonful cornstarch

(a) Remove the skin from the pike and take out the bones. Run through the grinder three times.
(b) Cut into small pieces the almonds, ham, and the vegetables.
(c) Put the pike into a big bowl and mix with it the cornstarch, 1 cup of water and 1 teaspoonful salt. Stir well for an hour. Be sure to stir in the same direction all the time.
(d) Add the nuts and ham. Mix well.
(e) Wash your hands as clean as possible. Hold the mixture in your hand and squeeze gently; a small ball will come through the top of the fingers, as

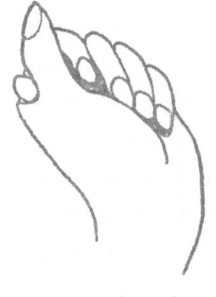

shown in the figure. Take off with a spoon. Wash the spoon each time with cold water.

(f) Place the ball in a pan of boiling water. When it comes to the top it indicates it is done and can be placed in a bowl.

(g) Cook the vegetables until done.

(h) Mix together the fish balls, the vegetables and Chinese gravy.

Fried Fish Balls

GUR YUE YUN

6 pounds pike
1½ cups salted almonds or peanuts
½ cup Chinese ham
6 pounds vegetables in season
1 teaspoonful cornstarch
2 cups mushrooms

(a) Remove the skin from the pike and take out the bones. Run through the grinder three times.

(b) Cut into small pieces the almonds, ham, and the vegetables.

(c) Put the pike into a big bowl and mix with it the cornstarch, 1 cup of water and 1 teaspoonful salt. Stir well for an hour. Be sure to stir in the same direction all the time.

(d) Add the nuts and ham. Mix well.

(e) Make the fish balls as described on the preceding page. Add a beaten egg, and boil in boiling oil until they turn yellow.

(f) Cook the vegetables and mushrooms until done.

(g) Mix together the fish balls, the vegetables, and Chinese gravy.

Raw Fish Party

YUE SANG

7 pounds pike
6 pounds carrots
2 cups green peppers
2 pieces ginger root
1 cup Chinese Chow Chow
A few lemon leaves
1 tablespoonful lemon juice
1 tablespoonful fried sesamum-seed

1 teaspoonful powdered salted almonds
1 teaspoonful powdered salted peanuts
S tablespoonfuls peanut oil
1 tablespoonful vinegar
2 cups chrysanthemums

(a) Remove the skin from the fish and take out the bones. Cut into pieces 1/16 inch by 1 inch by 1½ inches. Dry with a clean cloth.
(b) Cut into pieces 1/16 inch by 1/16 inch by 1½ inches the carrots, green peppers, ginger root. Chow Chow, and lemon leaves.
(c) Put the carrots into a suitable bag and squeeze all the juice out of them.
(d) Put the vinegar and a little salt in a large bowl. Add enough of the carrot and mix well with oil.
(e) Mix the vinegar, oil, peanut powder, and almond powder.
(f) Spread this mixture on top of the fish, and salt. Add the remaining vegetables. Then add oil and mix well.

Fried Fish

JOUT YUE

6 pounds pike or any fresh water fish
1 cup vinegar
1 teaspoonful cornstarch

(a) When the fish has been cleaned, rub inside and out with salt. Then fry in boiling oil until it turns brown.
(b) Add enough water to cover. Stir in the vinegar and the cornstarch. Cook for 10 minutes.
(c) Add Chinese gravy.

Hot Water Fish

NG LOW YUE

10 pounds cod
1 can Chinese Chow Chow
1 cup vinegar
2 teaspoonfuls salt

(a) Clean the cod but do not cut it.
(b) Pour into a bowl, boiling water equal to 5 times the weight of the fish. Add the salt. Place the fish in this and keep covered until the water gets lukewarm.

(c) Put the fish on a suitable plate and pour over it the gravy made of the Chow Chow, vinegar, and a little sugar, cornstarch, and salt.

Garnish with parsley and serve.

Steamed Pike

JING YUE

5 pounds pike
2 pieces Chinese onion
1 cup Chinese mushrooms
100 threads ginger root
The same amount of pork

(a) Clean the fish but do not cut it. Rub with salt. Add 1 teaspoonful oil.
(b) Cut the onion, mushrooms, ginger root, and pork into threads, 1½ inches long. Spread this on top of the fish and steam for ½ hour.
Garnish with parsley.

Eel

Eel in Net

MORN SEEN

4 pounds eel
1½ cups skinless chestnuts
1 teaspoonful Fun Wine
White of 1 egg
Lard (leaf lard) enough to wrap the eel

(a) Put the eel into warm water for 20 minutes. Take out and wash. Cut into pieces 1 inch long. Place in boiling oil and fry until yellow.
(b) Wrap each fried piece of eel with the lard. (This lard is the fat of a pig and looks like net.) Use the white of egg for paste.
(c) Put the wrapped eel into a pan. Add two cups more than enough water to cover. Add the chestnuts and Fun Wine. Cook until nearly dry (with about 2 cups of liquid remaining).
(d) Add Chinese gravy. Garnish with parsley.

Turtle

Steamed Turtle

DON QUY

    3 turtles
    2 cups mushrooms
    2 cups chestnuts
    ½ pound Chinese roast pork
    ½ cup Fun Wine
    1 teaspoonful ginger root juice

    (a) Put the live turtles into a cooking-pan of cold water. Bring to a boil slowly.
    (b) Remove the shell and interior. Wash. Cut the meat into pieces 1 inch by 1 inch by 1½ inches.
    (c) Have a hot fire. Put 2 tablespoonfuls of oil into a frying-pan. When the oil is very hot put in the meat, Fun Wine, and ginger root juice. Fry for 10 minutes. Turn constantly.
    (d) Cut the bamboo shoots into pieces ¾ inch by 1½ inches by 1/16 inch. Cut the pork Into pieces ¾ inch by 1½ inches by ¾ inch.
    (e) Add to the meat in the frying-pan, the mushrooms, chestnuts, bamboo shoots, pork and enough primary soup to cover. Bring to a boil.
    (f) Put all into a suitable bowl and steam for 1¾ hours.
    (g) Skim off any oil which may be on the top. Salt to taste. Not only the meat is delicious but the soup also.

Turtle Soup

QUY TONG

    3 turtles
    2 cups mushrooms
    2 cups chestnuts
    ½ pound Chinese roast pork
    ½ cup Fun Wine
    1 teaspoonful ginger root juice
    25 cents' worth of Bug Kay

    (a) Put the live turtles into a cooking-pan of cold water. Bring to a boil slowly.

(b) Remove the shell and interior. Wash. Cut the meat into pieces 1 inch by 1 inch by 1½ inches.

(c) Have a hot fire. Put 2 tablespoonfuls of oil into a frying-pan. When the oil is very hot put in the meat, Fun Wine, and ginger root juice. Fry for 10 minutes. Turn constantly,

{d) Cut the bamboo shoots into pieces ¾ inch by 1½ inches by 1/16 inch. Cut the pork into pieces ½ inch by 1½ inches by ¾ inch.

(e) Add to the meat in the frying-pan, the mushrooms, chestnuts, bamboo shoots, pork and enough primary soup to cover. Bring to a boil.

(f) Put into a suitable bowl, add the Bug Kay, Dong Sum, Gay Gee, Yen York and steam for 1¾ hours.

(g) Skim off any oil which may be on the top. Salt to taste. Serve the soup in bowls.

Bug Kay is a plant and can be bought in any Chinese grocery store. It is used both for nourishment and for its flavor. Bug Kay and Dong Sum look like wooden sticks and must be removed before the soup is served.

Shark

Shark Fins

YUE CHE

This dish has an interesting history. A ruler of China found a large shark in the South Sea. It was killed. Later, in deciding how best to use each part of the animal, a cook by the name of Lang Pow invented this dish. He discovered how delicious and tasty it was. This was in the year 50 B.C.

Shark fins are prepared as follows:

The fins and tails are steeped in boiling water for ½ hour. The skin is then scraped off with a knife; and the fins and tails are boiled for an hour or until they fall to pieces. Every piece of meat, skin, and bone is then removed. Only what is left, a fin soft yellow in color, is kept. This is dried and sold from two to three dollars a pound as shark fins.

(a) Buy 2 pounds of dry shark fins from a Chinese grocery store. Soak in cold water for 3 hours.

(b) Boil the fins with a few pieces of dry garlic and 2 pieces of ginger root. Change the water several times when boiling.

(c) Put into a suitable pan. Add 2 tablespoonfuls of lard, and twice more than enough primary soup to cover. Boil slowly for ½ hour. Drain off the liquid and throw it away.

(d) Put into another pan, containing 6 pints of primary soup, and boil.

(e) Change again into a third pan of primary soup. Add gravy which consists of 1 cup of chicken starch, the whites of 3 eggs, Chinese ham dice and a little cornstarch and salt. Use 1 tablespoonful red vinegar to improve the taste. Garnish with parsley and serve hot.

Shrimp

Shrimp Chop Suey

CHOW HAR YUN

2 pounds shrimp with the shells off
2 cups dry mushrooms
2 cups bean sprouts
1 piece of onion cut into threads
½ teaspoonful Fun Wine

(a) Fry mushrooms, bean sprouts, and onion in an oily pan for 10 minutes. Add enough water to cover. Boil for 15 minutes.
(b) Fry the shrimp in a hot, oiled pan and add the Fun Wine. Keep frying until the shrimp turns red.
(c) Mix the shrimp with the mushrooms, bean sprouts, and onion, and add 2 cups of primary soup. When it boils, add Chinese gravy.

Steadied Shrimp

DON HAR

24 large shrimps
48 pieces bamboo shoots
1 tablespoonful Fun Wine
1 teaspoonful ginger root juice

(a) Remove the shells from the shrimps and cut into halves. Fry in a hot oiled pan.
(b) Mix together the Fun Wine and the ginger root juice. Add this liquid to the shrimps. Cook for 5 minutes. Drain off the liquid but do not throw it away.
(c) The 48 pieces of bamboo shoots should be the same size as the halves of the shrimp, 1/16 inch long. Place the shrimp and bamboo shoots in a bowl, arranging them — first a piece of shrimp and then a piece of bamboo shoot, and so on — having them parallel.

(d) Add ½ cup primary soup and steam for 2 hours.
(e) Turn now into another bowl by placing the two bowls mouth to mouth. Add gravy and serve.

Fried Shrimp

JOUT HAR

2 pounds shrimp
2 pounds green peppers
2 eggs
1 tablespoonful cornstarch

(a) Mix up the shrimp, eggs and cornstarch. Add salt to suit the taste. Put one by one into a pan of boiling oil. Fry until brown.
(b) Cut the green peppers into pieces the same size as the shrimp. Fry in an oiled pan for 2 minutes. Then add the shrimp and mix well,
(c) Add enough primary soup to cover. Cook for 10 minutes.
(d) Add Chinese gravy. Garnish with parsley and serve.

Oysters

Oyster Chop Suey

CHOW HO SE PIN

2 dozen oysters
9 cups bamboo shoots
2 cups water chestnuts
2 cups celery
A few pieces of pork
1 tablespoonful Fun Wine
1 teaspoonful ginger juice

(a) Cut the oysters, bamboo shoots, chestnuts, celery, and pork into fragments.
(b) Put the oysters into boiling water for 10 minutes. Then fry the oysters in a hot oiled pan.
(c) Add the Fun Wine and the ginger juice. Continue to cook for 5 minutes.
(d) Fry the bamboo shoots, water chestnuts, celery, and pork in an oiled pan for 5 minutes. Add to oysters.

(e) Add 1 cup primary soup and boil until about 1 cup of liquid remains.
(f) Add Chinese gravy.

Steadied Oysters

DON HO SE

2½ dozen oysters
Lard-skin (enough to wrap the oysters)
1 teaspoonful ginger juice
1 tablespoonful Fun Wine
Whites of 2 eggs

(a) Wash the oysters. Boil them in water for 10 minutes. Then fry in hot oil.
(b) Add the Fun Wine and ginger juice. Fry for 7 minutes.
(c) Cut the lard-skin into pieces as wide as the oysters and about 4 inches long. Wrap each oyster with a piece of lard-skin, using the white of egg for paste.
(d) Put the wrapped oysters into boiling oil and fry until they are brown.
(e) Now set them in a bowl and steam for 1½ hours.
Serve on lettuce.

Roasted Oysters

SU HO SEE

2½ dozen oysters
1 cup red vinegar
Sesamum-seed oil
Sugar
Salt

(a) Dry the oysters with a clean, dry cloth. Then dip in oil.
(b) String the oysters through a wire and roast until done over a charcoal fire. Have them about 1 foot above the fire.
Serve with a sauce made of the red vinegar, sesamum-seed oil, sugar, and salt.

Lobster

Lobster Chop Suey

CHOW LUNG HAR PIN

1 lobster (about 6 pounds)
2 cups bamboo shoots
2 cups water chestnuts
2 cups celery
A few pieces of Chinese onion
1 tablespoonful Fun Wine
1 teaspoonful ginger root juice

(a) Boil the lobster in water until it turns red. Take off the shell and cut the meat into fragments not longer than 1½ inches.

(b) Fry the lobster with the Fun Wine, and ginger root juice for 5 minutes over a hot fire.

(c) Cut the bamboo shoots, water chestnuts, celery, and onion into pieces the size of the lobster fragments. Fry these in a hot, oiled pan for 3 minutes. Add water enough to cover and cook for 10 minutes. Then mix with the lobster.

(d) When there is about 1 cup of liquid left, add Chinese gravy, mix well, and serve.

Crab

HI

Crabs are found most abundantly in salt water. The best quality is found in a place where the salt and fresh water mix. Although they exist all the year round, the best months for crabs are February, July, and August. In buying crabs always look for the heavy ones. The light ones contain too much water.

Naturally the most delicious food is crab. This is the only meat which contains enough salt and oil to fit any one's taste.

In cooking crab, therefore, all that is necessary is to wash and steam it until the crab turns red. Serve when hot. Sometimes red vinegar is used in serving but it is not necessary.

Never add salt or oil or butter of any kind because it spoils the flavor.

Crab Soup

HI TONG

6 crabs
1 cup water chestnuts
1 cup bamboo shoots
1 cup mushrooms
7 pints primary soup

(a) Remove the shells from the crabs and put into boiling water for ½ hour. By means of a fork take out the meat and break into small pieces.
(b) Cut secondary vegetables into pieces. Cook for 20 minutes.
(c) Now put the secondary vegetables in with the crab.
(d) Add primary soup and cook for 15 minutes.
(e) Add Chinese gravy, mix well, and remove from the stove at once. Stir in parsley and garnish.

Fried Soft-Shell Crab

OUT YUN HORK HI

6 soft-shell crabs
2 eggs
1 cup red vinegar
1 tablespoonful cornstarch

(a) Mix the crab with the cornstarch and eggs. Salt to taste.
(b) Fry in boiling oil until golden brown.
Serve with the red vinegar.

Chinese Tomato

Fried Chinese Tomato with Crab

HI SUE KAR

6 crabs
Chinese tomato equal in weight to crabs, including shell
1 tablespoonful Fun Wine
½ teaspoonful ginger juice
1 cup primary soup

(a) Wash the crabs. Open the shell. Steam until they turn red. By means of a fork take off all the meat. Tear it into small pieces.

(b) Fry the tomato in boiling oil until it turns yellow. Then mash into starch.

(c) Fry the crab in a hot, oiled pan.

(d) Add ginger juice and Fun Wine. Turn often.

(e) Add the tomato. Mix well.

(f) Add the primary soup. When all is dry, remove from the stove at once.

(g) Add salt and red vinegar to improve the taste.

Garnish with parsley.

Fried Chinese Tomato with Shrimp

HAR SUE KAR

3 pounds shrimp
6 pounds Chinese tomato
1 tablespoonful Fun Wine
½ teaspoonful ginger juice
1 cup primary soup

(a) Fry the shrimp in a hot, oiled pan.

(b) Fry the tomato in boiling oil until it turns yellow. Then mash into starch.

(c) Add ginger juice and Fun Wine. Turn often,

(d) Add the tomato. Mix well.

(e) Add the primary soup. When all is dry, remove from the stove at once.

(f) Add salt and red vinegar to improve the taste.

Garnish with parsley.

Pigeon

Why Shon Pigeon

WHY SHON YUE GOB

6 pigeons
A few pieces of pork
10 cents' worth of Kee Zee
25 cents' worth of Dong Chong Chow
10 cents' worth of Why Shon

This dish not only is nutritious and pleasing to the taste, but it also has great value as a medicine. Physicians often advise sick people to eat *Why Shon Yue Gob*. Its benefits and the results of its use in rebuilding the strength of convalescent people are wonderful and indescribable.

(a) When the pigeons have been washed, rub inside and out with salt. Put in a bowl.

(b) Wash the Why Shon, Kee Zee, Dong Chong Chow, and pork. Add to the pigeons.

(c) Cover with primary soup and steam for 1¾ hours in a double-boiler.

(d) Remove the oil from the top of the liquid. Salt to taste. Use the liquid for soup.

Serve the pigeon with oil and Chinese sauce.

Pigeon Chop Suey

CHOW YUE GOB

6 pigeons
2 cups water chestnuts
2 cups bamboo shoots
2 cups mushrooms
2 cups celery
2 cups primary soup

(a) Take the bones out of the pigeons and cut the meat into thin pieces. Put into a hot, oiled pan and fry for 5 minutes.

(b) Cut the secondary vegetables into thin pieces. Put into a hot pan and fry for 2 minutes. Add water and cook for 15 minutes.

(c) Add the secondary vegetables to the pigeon fragments. Mix well.

(d) Add primary soup and cook for 5 minutes.

(e) Add Chinese gravy.

Bird-Nest in Pigeon

GOB TON YIN

6 pigeons
2 cups bird-nest
1 cup primary soup
1 piece of ginger root

(a) Soak the bird-nest in cold water for 1 hour. Shake off any feathers, etc. Wash gently and boil for 1¾ hours with the ginger.

(b) Pick the pigeons. Chop off the head, feet and wings. Cut one line 3 inches long and take out the interior. Wash the pigeons and rub inside and out with salt. Place in a bowl with the cut side on top.

(c) Fill the pigeons with the bird-nest and primary soup. Steam for 2¼ hours in a double-boiler.

(d) Now transfer into a larger bowl by putting the two bowls mouth to mouth.

Garnish with Chinese ham dice.

Fried Pigeon

SUE YE GOB

Clean 6 young pigeons, or squabs, and put them into a bowl of Chinese sauce. Fry in boiling oil until yellow. Serve when hot with spicery salt.

Pigeon Hash

YE GOB SONG

4 pigeons
2 cups water chestnuts
2 cups mushrooms
2 cups bamboo shoots
½ teaspoonful ginger juice
1 teaspoonful Fun Wine
1 head of lettuce
1 tablespoonful ham dice
1 cup fried noodles

(a) Cut into very small pieces the pigeons, water chestnuts, mushrooms, and bamboo shoots. Cut the lettuce into threads.

(b) Fry the chopped pigeon in a hot, oiled pan.

(c) Add the ginger juice and Fun Wine.

(d) Add the vegetables and mix well.

(e) Add enough primary soup to cover and cook until done.

(f) Add Chinese gravy and remove from the stove at once. Salt to suit the taste.

Serve on top of the lettuce. Use the Chinese ham dice and fried noodles as a garnish.

Quail

Quail Hash

ARM CHUN SONG

4 quails
2 cups water chestnuts
2 cups mushrooms
2 cups bamboo shoots
½ teaspoonful ginger juice
1 teaspoonful Fun Wine
1 head of lettuce
1 tablespoonful ham dice
1 cup fried noodles

(a) Cut the quail, water chestnuts, mushrooms, and bamboo shoots into very small pieces. Cut the lettuce into threads.
(b) Fry the chopped quails in a hot, oiled pan.
(c) Add the secondary vegetables and mix well.
(d) Add enough primary soup to cover and cook until done.
(e) Add Chinese gravy and remove from the stove at once. Salt to suit the taste.
Serve on top of the lettuce. Use the Chinese ham dice and fried noodles as a garnish.

Partridge

Partridge Hash

JAR QUO SONG

4 partridges
2 cups water chestnuts
2 cups mushrooms
2 cups bamboo shoots
½ teaspoonful ginger juice
1 teaspoonful Fun Wine
1 head lettuce
1 tablespoonful ham dice
1 cup fried noodles

(a) Cut the partridges, water chestnuts, mushrooms, and bamboo shoots into very small pieces. Cut the lettuce into threads.
(b) Fry the chopped partridges in a hot, oiled pan.
(c) Add the ginger juice and Fun Wine.
(d) Add the vegetables and mix well.
(e) Add enough primary soup to cover and cook until done.
(f) Add Chinese gravy and remove from the stove at once. Salt to suit the taste.

Serve on top of the lettuce. Use the Chinese ham dice and fried noodles as a garnish.

Partridge Chop Suey

CHOW JAR QUO

4 partridges
2 cups water chestnuts
5 cups mushrooms
2 cups celery
2 cups primary soup

(a) Take the bones out of the partridges and cut the meat into thin pieces. Put into a hot, oiled pan and fry for 5 minutes.
(b) Cut the secondary vegetables into thin pieces. Put into a hot pan and fry for 2 minutes. Add water and cook for 15 minutes.
(c) Add the secondary vegetables to the partridge fragments. Mix well.
(d) Add primary soup and cook for 5 minutes.
(e) Add Chinese gravy.

Why Shon Partridge

WHY SHON JAR QUO

6 partridges
A few pieces of pork
10 cents' worth of Why Shon
10 cents' worth of Kee Zee
25 cents' worth of Dong Chong Chow

(a) When the partridges have been washed, rub inside and out with salt. Put in a bowl.
(b) Wash the Why Shon, Kee Zee, Dong Chong Chow, and pork. Add to the partridges.

(c) Cover with primary soup and steam for 3¾ hours in a double-boiler.

(d) Remove the oil from the top of the liquid. Salt to taste. Use the liquid for soup.

Serve the partridge with oil and Chinese sauce.

Deer

LOCK YOK

2 pounds deer
2 cups water chestnuts
2 cups mushrooms
2 cups bamboo shoots
1 pound chicken meat
½ teaspoonful ginger juice
1 tablespoonful Fun Wine
A few pieces of sugar-cane about 3 inches long, unskinned

(a) Cut the deer into pieces 1½ inches by 1½ inches by 1 inch. Cut the secondary vegetables into small pieces.

(b) Fry the deer in a hot, oiled pan. Turn constantly.

(c) Add the ginger juice, sugar-cane, and a little salt. Add the secondary vegetables and the chicken and cook for 5 minutes.

(d) Add enough primary soup to cover and bring to a boil.

(e) Transfer to a suitable bowl. Put the Fun Wine on top. Steam for 2 hours. Serve with oil and Chinese sauce.

Goose

Roast Goose

SUE OR

1 goose
1 teaspoonful spicery powder
1 cup Chinese sauce
A few drops sesamum-seed oil
1 teaspoonful salt

(a) Put the goose in hot, not boiling, water for 2 minutes and then add the spicery powder, sauce, oil, and the salt. Leave the goose in for 20 minutes. Be sure every bit of goose is dipped into it.

(b) Place the goose, as shown in cut depicting the Chinese roasting stove. Start the fire before this, so that the wall is hot. Let the goose roast for 1 hour. A hot fire is necessary before the goose is put in. Afterward have a low fire. There must be no smoke.

Winkle

CHOW HUNG LOR

3 winkles
2 cups water chestnuts, unshelled
2 cups mushrooms
2 cups bamboo shoots
1 cup celery
A few pieces of pork
½ teaspoonful ginger root juice
1 tablespoonful Fun Wine
1 cup primary soup

(a) Wash the winkles carefully. Break the shell. Take the meat out. Cut into pieces 1/16 inch by 1½ inches by 1½ inches.
(b) Cut the secondary vegetables and the pork into pieces and fry in a hot, oiled pan. Add enough water to cover. Cover the pan and cook until done.
(c) Fry the meat over a quick fire in a hot, oiled pan. Add the ginger root juice and the Fun Wine.
(d) Now add the secondary vegetables and mix well.
(e) Add the primary soup and Chinese gravy.
Serve with Chinese ham dice and parsley for garnish.

Eggs

Plain Omelet

CHOW DON

12 eggs
A little oil
Salt
Chinese ham dice
Parsley

(a) Break the eggs in a bowl. Add oil and salt. Beat well.

(b) Put plenty of oil in a hot frying-pan. Be sure that every part of the pan is covered with oil.

(c) Have a medium fire. Place the eggs in the pan and keep turning with a cooking-shovel.

(d) When the omelet is done add the Chinese ham dice and parsley for garnish.

Pork Omelet

FO YUNG YORK

12 eggs
1 pound pork
2 onions
2 cups bamboo shoots
2 cups water chestnuts

Twelve eggs, a little oil, salt, Chinese ham dice, parsley.

(a) Beat the eggs well and put them in a bowl with oil and salt.

(b) Cut the onions, pork, bamboo shoots, and water chestnuts into threads 1½ inches long.

(c) Mix together all of the ingredients and fry in boiling oil until done.

(d) Put all in a bowl and add Chinese gravy.

Chicken Omelet

FO YUN GUY

12 eggs
1½ pounds chicken
2 onions
2 cups bamboo shoots
2 cups water chestnuts
2 cups mushrooms

(a) Beat the eggs well and put them in a bowl with oil and salt.

(b) Cut the onions, chicken, bamboo shoots, water chestnuts, and mushrooms into threads 1½ inches long.

(c) Mix together all of the ingredients and fry in boiling oil until done.

(d) Put all in a bowl and add Chinese gravy.

Shrimp Omelet

FO YUNG HAR

12 eggs
1 pound shrimp
2 onions
2 cups bamboo shoots
2 cups water chestnuts
2 cups mushrooms

(a) Beat the eggs well and put them in a bowl with oil and salt.
(b) Cut the onions, shrimp, bamboo shoots, water chestnuts, and mushrooms into threads 1½ inches long.
(c) Mix together all of the ingredients and fry in boiling oil until done.
(d) Put all in a bowl and add Chinese gravy.

Crab Omelet

FO YUNG HIGH

6 crabs
12 eggs
2 onions
2 cups bamboo shoots
2 cups water chestnuts
2 cups mushrooms

(a) Beat the eggs well and put them in a bowl with oil and salt.
(b) Cut the onions, crabs, bamboo shoots, water chestnuts, and mushrooms into threads 1½ inches long.
(c) Mix together all of the ingredients and fry in boiling oil until done.
(d) Put all in a bowl and add Chinese gravy.

Lobster Omelet

FO YUNG LUNG HA

3 pounds lobster
12 eggs
2 cups bamboo shoots
2 cups water chestnuts
2 cups mushrooms
2 onions

(a) Beat the eggs well in a bowl with oil and salt.
(b) Cut the onions, lobster, bamboo shoots, water chestnuts, and mushrooms into threads 1½ inches long. Cook until done.
(c) Add beaten eggs and mix well. Continue to cook until eggs are done.

Bean Cake Omelet

FO YUNG DOW FO

12 eggs
A little oil
Salt
6 pieces bean cake
Chinese ham dice
Parsley

(a) Beat the eggs with a little salt and oil.
(b) Fry the bean cakes in an oiled pan. Add water and boil for 10 minutes.
(c) Put plenty of oil in the pan, greasing it well all over. Put in the egg. Keep on turning until nearly done. Add the bean cake and cook until done.
Use Chinese ham dice and parsley for garnish.

Fried Eggs

YOUT JAR DON

12 eggs
1 cup dried mushrooms
1½ pounds chicken
A few Chinese onions
A piece of ginger root

(a) Boil the eggs until hard. Take off the shell without destroying the shape of the eggs. Now fry them in boiling oil.
(b) Cut the mushrooms, chicken, bamboo shoots, and ginger root into threads 1½ inches long. Fry for 5 minutes in a hot, oiled pan.
(c) Pour this over the eggs. Add twice more than enough primary soup to cover and cook until 2 cups of liquid remain.
(d) Add Chinese gravy.
Serve with parsley as a garnish.

Egg Roll

DAN GUN

6 eggs
2 tablespoonfuls dry mushrooms
2 tablespoonfuls bean sprouts
2 tablespoonfuls chicken meat
2 tablespoonfuls Chinese ham

(a) Break the eggs into a bowl. Beat well with oil and salt. Have a low fire. Oil pan. Place in it one tablespoonful of well-beaten egg. Take hold of the pan and let the egg run all over the surface of the pan. A layer of egg will be formed.

(b) Cut the mushrooms, Chinese ham, bean sprouts, and chicken into threads. Fry for 5 minutes in an oiled pan. Salt to suit the taste. Add enough water to cover and cook until dry. When nearly dry, turn constantly to prevent burning.

(c) Roll this in the egg, making the roll 1 inch in diameter and as long as the egg layer. Use white of egg for paste. Cut carefully into the desired length.

(d) Add Chinese gravy.

Checker-Board Eggs

KA GE DON

12 eggs
1 tablespoonful Chinese ham
2 cups bamboo shoots
1 cup celery
1 cup water chestnuts

(a) Cut the ham and secondary vegetables into threads 1½ inches long. Fry in an oiled pan. Mix well. Add enough primary soup to cover. Cook until done. Salt to suit the taste.

(b) Beat the eggs well with oil and salt. Put them into a hot pan and let them run all over the pan evenly. Turn over.

(c) Put this egg layer on a dish. Cover one-half of the layer with the fried ham, bamboo shoot, celery, and water chestnuts about ½ inch thick. Then cover this with the other half of the egg layer.

(d) Add Chinese gravy.

Fish Roll

YEE YORK DAN GUN

   6 eggs
   4 pounds pike
   1 tablespoonful Chinese ham
   1 cup peanuts, pounded
   1 cup Chinese roast pork

(a) Break the eggs into a bowl. Beat well with oil and salt. Have a low fire. Oil pan. Place into it 1 tablespoonful well beaten egg. Take hold of the pan and let the egg run over the surface of the pan. A layer of egg will be formed.

(b) Remove the skin from the pike and take out the bones. Grind the meat through a fine grinder several times, or pound with a hammer as fine as possible. Beat well for ¾ hour with salt and a small amount of oil.

(c) Cut the Chinese ham and pork into dice. Mix well with the remaining egg, the pike, and the peanuts.

(d) Roll this mixture into the egg layer, having the layer 1 inch in diameter. Steam for ½ hour.

(e) Cut into the desired length and add Chinese gravy.

Gold and Silver Egg

GOM NON DON

   12 eggs
   3 pounds pike
   1 tablespoonful Chinese ham

(a) Break the eggs carefully. Put the whites in one bowl and the yolks in another bowl. To each bowl add an equal amount of cold, boiled water and mix well.

(b) Grind or hammer the pike (with skin and bones removed). Beat with a little water. Mix well with the whites of the eggs. Salt to suit the taste.

(c) Chop the Chinese ham into pieces as small as possible. Mix with the yolks of the eggs. Salt to suit the taste.

{d) Now put the Chinese ham on one side of the dish and the pike on the other side. Do not let them mix. Steam for 20 minutes. When done there will be gold color on one side of the dish and silver on the other side.

Add oil and parsley before serving.

Stuffed Egg

YUNG DON

6 eggs
Shrimp or crab meat chopped fine
Chinese ham, diced
Chicken, chopped fine
Water chestnuts or Chinese onions chopped fine

(The amount of meat and water chestnuts combined should be one-half the volume of the yolks of the eggs.)

(a) Oil enough egg cups. Break the eggs carefully into these, putting in the whites first. Now put the unbeaten yolk in the center of the cup, letting it float on top. Steam the eggs until done.

(b) With a spoon carefully take off the yolk of the egg,

(c) Fill the egg with the chicken and other ingredients, well mixed. Steam about 20 minutes.

Serve with sesamum-seed oil and sauce.

Fish Swimming in a Golden Pond

YUE YORK JING DON

7 eggs
2 pounds pike
1 tablespoonful Chinese ham dice

(a) Remove the skin from the pike. Cut the meat into small pieces.

(b) Mix the eggs with an equal amount of cold, boiled water. Beat well. Salt to suit the taste.

(c) Put the eggs in a suitable bowl. Spread the pike on top. Steam for 20 minutes.

Garnish with the ham and parsley, and serve with oil and sauce.

Shrimp in Golden Pond

HAR JING DON

7 eggs
1 pound shrimp
1 tablespoonful Chinese ham dice

(a) Remove the skin from the shrimp. Cut the meat into small pieces.

(b) Mix the eggs with an equal amount of cold, boiled water. Beat well. Salt to suit the taste.

(c) Put the eggs in a suitable bowl. Spread the shrimp on top. Steam for 20 minutes.

Garnish with the ham and parsley, and serve with oil and sauce.

Crab in Golden Pond

HI JOK JING DON

7 eggs
3 pounds crab
1 tablespoonful Chinese ham dice

(a) Remove the shell from the crab. Cut the meat into small pieces.

(b) Mix the eggs with an equal amount of cold, boiled water. Beat well. Salt to suit the taste.

(c) Put the eggs in a suitable bowl. Spread the crab on top. Steam for 20 minutes.

Garnish with the ham and parsley, and serve with oil and sauce.

Lobster in Golden Pond

LUNG HA JING DON

7 eggs
3 pounds lobster
1 tablespoonful Chinese ham dice

(a) Remove the shell from the lobster. Cut the meat into small pieces.

(b) Mix the eggs with an equal amount of cold, boiled water. Beat well. Salt to suit the taste.

(c) Put the eggs in a suitable bowl. Spread the lobster on top. Steam for 20 minutes.

Garnish with the ham and parsley, and serve with oil and sauce.

Beans

Bean Sprouts

AR CHOY

Soak some beans in water in a flat dish. Spread the beans out; do not let one cover another.

Cover with a piece of wet cloth, and water every morning. The sprouts will appear in two nights.

They are ready to eat when they are 2 inches long.

Bean sprouts are palatable and very nutritious.

Bean Cake

DO FO

This is a most delicious dish for its price. Many people in Paris can tell you how delicious it is, for there is a factory in Paris which makes millions of dollars each year by manufacturing this cake.

The process of making bean cake is really so complicated that it would require a separate volume to describe it.

Put white beans in cold water for a few hours. Then grind in a water stone-grinder. Cook for 5 hours with calcium powder. Let it filter through a cloth and run into a cup or bowl. When cool it becomes solid. Tie this in a piece of cloth and boil. This is called bean cake.

Bean Cake Chop Suey

DO FO JAP

1½ pounds pork
10 pieces bean cake
2 cups onions

(a) Cut the pork, bean cake, and the onions into small pieces.
(b) Put them into an oiled pan and fry for 10 minutes.
(c) Add enough water to cover. Cover the pan and cook for 15 minutes.
(d) Add Chinese gravy.
Serve hot, in individual bowls.

Chicken Starch Bean Cake

GUY YUNG DO FO

Chicken starch is made by pounding chicken, without the skin and bone, as fine as possible. It is best to pound it with a hammer on a chopping-board. Add to this 1 teaspoonful of cornstarch, white of an egg, and one cup of primary soup. Stir well.

In using chicken starch, always pour it into the substance before placing the pan on the stove. Keep stirring. Take the pan away from the fire just as it begins to boil. The flavor is bad if it boils too long.

(a) Fry five pieces of bean cake in boiling oil for 5 minutes. Cut them into ¼ inch cubes. Put in cold water until no oil floats on the top.

(b) Mix well the bean cake with one-half as much Chinese ham dice and an equal amount of milk. Cook in a pan until just done.

(c) Add the chicken starch, and sugar to suit the taste. Watch the heat carefully so that the chicken starch will not be too well done.

Stuffed Triangle Bean Cake

YUNG DO FO

12 bean cakes
3 pounds pike
½ cup Chinese ham dice
½ cup Chinese onion dice
½ cup salted almonds

Bean cakes come in pieces about 2 inches by 2 inches. Cut each cake into two triangles, as shown in the figure. Now cut the triangles as in figure *b*. Remove the pieces as in *c*. Leave the hole as shown in figure *d*.

(a) Grind or pound the pike. Stir up in a small amount of salt water for ½ hour.

(b) Mix with the ham, onions, and almonds.

(c) Fill the hole in the bean cake with this mixture. Fry in boiling oil until yellow.

(d) Cook the fried bean cake triangles in primary soup for ½ hour.

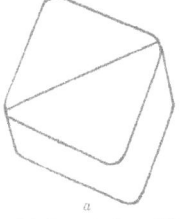

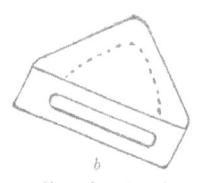

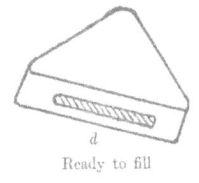

(e) Add a gravy made of Chinese sauce, a few drops of sesamum-seed oil, sweet sauce, and cornstarch.

Garnish with parsley.

Ruby Mixed with Pearls

FOR TOY DO FO GUY NUP

9 bean cakes
1 pound of Chinese ham
1 pound of shrimp

(a) Remove the thin outer layer from the bean cakes.
(b) Cut the ham and the shrimp into ¼ inch cubes.
(c) Boil all together in a pan of primary soup until the shrimp turns red.
(d) Add Chinese gravy. Garnish with parsley.

Bean Biscuit

DO SAR BOW

1 pound red beans
2 pounds flour
½ cup lard
1 teaspoonful salt
2 teaspoonfuls baking powder

(a) Cook the beans in water for 3 hours, and mash. Place in water so that the skins of the beans float on top. Remove these and then filter the beans through a thick cloth and let dry. Now mix with the lard and a little sugar.
(b) Sift the flour and mix with it enough cold water to make a thin dough.
(c) Roll the dough out thin. Cut in the size of biscuits.
(d) Now roll these biscuits flat and fill each one with the beans, wrapping the dough around the beans to make a perfect ball. Close the dough up carefully.
(e) Let the dough biscuits stand in a double-boiler for 10 minutes before putting on the fire. Steam for ¾ hour.

Stuffed Squash

YUNG CHIN GUAR

1 squash
3 pounds pike, ground
2 tablespoonfuls Chinese ham dice
2 Chinese onions, diced
½ cup salted almonds, diced

(a) Put the pike in a small amount of salt water and stir for ½ hour. Then mix with the ham, onions, and almonds.

(b) Remove the seeds from the squash and fill with the pike, ham, etc. Fry in boiling oil until yellow.

(c) Cook in primary soup for ½ hour.

(d) Add a gravy made of Chinese sauce, a few drops of sesamum-seed oil, sweet sauce, and cornstarch.

Garnish with parsley.

Stuffed Green Peppers

YUNG LAR CHU

18 green peppers
3 pounds pike, ground
2 tablespoonfuls Chinese ham dice
2 Chinese onions, diced
½ cup salted almonds, diced

(a) Put the pike in a small amount of salt water and stir for ½ hour. Then mix with the ham, onions, and almonds.

(b) Cut the peppers into halves, take out the seeds, and fill with the pike, ham, etc. Fry in boiling oil until yellow.

(c) Cook in primary soup for ½ hour.

(d) Add a gravy made of Chinese sauce, a few drops of sesamum-seed oil, sweet sauce, and cornstarch.

Garnish with parsley.

Immortal Food

JAI

Dr. Wu Tingfang, the former Ambassador from China to the United States, told his friends that he would return to America in fifty years. He said this as he left the United States. He was then over sixty years old. His reason for expecting long life is that he lives entirely on dishes which contain no meat.

Buddha said that if you leave meat alone you will live forever. Therefore the priests and nuns belonging to the Buddhist religion live on dishes which contain no meat.

There are many of these dishes.

Food of The God of Law Horn

LAW HORN JAI

12 pieces bean cake
2 cups white nuts
2 cups fungus
A few pieces of bean stick
2 cups bamboo shoots
2 cups dry mushrooms

(a) Cut each bean cake into 4 pieces. Fry in boiling oil until nicely brown. Put in cold water and change the water until no oil floats on the top.
(b) Soak the fungus, bean stick, and nuts in cold water for ½ hour.
(c) Cut the bamboo shoots into pieces 1½ inches by 1 inch by 1/16 inch.
(d) Put all the ingredients except the mushrooms into an oiled pan and cover with water. Cook for 1 hour.
(e) Add the mushrooms and cook for 15 minutes.
(f) Add Chinese gravy.

Soft Immortal Food

YUEN JAI

12 pieces bean cake
2 cups dry mushrooms
4 ounces Chinese vermicelli
A few bean sticks

(a) Cut each piece of bean cake into 4 pieces.

(b) Soak the mushrooms, vermicelli, and bean sticks in water for ½ hour. Cut the vermicelli into pieces 3 inches long.

(c) Put all of the ingredients in cold water and cook for 1 hour. Put in plenty of oil and red cheese.

(d) Add Chinese gravy.

Hard Immortal Food

ARN JAI

12 pieces bean cake
East melon (twice the amount of bean cake)
2 cups white nuts

(a) Cut each bean cake into 4 pieces. Cut the melon into pieces 1 inch by 1 inch by 1½ inches.

(b) Fry all in an oiled pan.

(c) Add enough water to cover. Add ¼ cake of red cheese and plenty of oil. Mix. Cook for 1 hour.

Dry Foods

LAB MAY

In ancient times the people preserved foods for future use. They would hunt in summer, store away the food, and eat it in winter. It is very important to store away food. In the European War, for instance, the English blockade cannot starve the Germans because they have plenty of stored foods. Dry foods are a necessity.

The Oriental people have the same idea as to storing foods and as to the sanitary preparation of these foods.

If the dry foods were not sanitary they could not be imported into America. Every food has to be examined by a doctor. All these prepared foods are certified by a doctor's certificate which is proof that they are sanitary.

Chinese Frankfurter

LAB CHUNG

(a) Get the outside lining of the small intestine of a pig. Wash thoroughly with salt and then put into hot water for 10 minutes. Tie one end, force air through from the other end, and tie. Dry in the hot sun.

(b) Cut pork into pieces ¾ inch by ¾ inch by ¾ inch. To every pound of pork add 3 ounces of salt, 1 tablespoonful of sweet sauce, 1 tablespoonful of Fun Wine, and a few threads of orange skin. Mix well.

(c) By means of a funnel, put this mixture into the pig lining. Tie the skin about every 6 inches. Punch plenty of small holes with a needle.

(d) Expose in the hot sun for 1 day. Put in a windy place for 4 days. The air should be dry, so it is best to make these in the fall or winter.

Chinese Frankfurter should be kept in a china jar. At least they must be kept in a jar for 5 days before being eaten.

Steam them in a double-boiler for ½ hour before serving. Serve with fried potatoes or fried gray potatoes underneath.

Chinese Frankfurters on Rice

LAB CHUNG BO FON

3 cups rice
6 pairs Chinese frankfurters

(a) Wash the rice 3 times. Put in a covered pan with 7½ cups water and cook until boiled.

(b) Place the Chinese frankfurters on top of the rice. When dry keep over a low fire. Move the pan frequently to prevent burning. Take from the stove and keep the cover on for 10 minutes.

(c) Take out the Chinese frankfurters and cut into the required size.

(d) Add salt, mix well.

This makes a very dainty winter breakfast. The juice from the frankfurters gives the rice a delicious flavor.

Chinese Frankfurters with Vegetables

CHOY CHOW LAB CHUNG

9 pairs Chinese frankfurters
Any Chinese vegetables (twice the amount of the frankfurters)

(a) Cut the vegetables into pieces 1 inch by 1 inch by 1½ inches. Fry in an oiled pan with salt until the volume is considerably reduced. Add water enough to cover.

(b) Add the frankfurters. Cover and cook until nearly dry.

(c) Add Chinese gravy.

Lamb Frankfurters

YUNG YORK CHUNG

(a) Get the outside lining of the small intestine of a pig. Wash thoroughly with salt and then put into hot water for 10 minutes. Tie one end, force air through from the other end, and tie. Dry in the hot sun.

(b) Cut lamb into pieces ¾ inch by ¾ inch by ¾ inch. To every pound of lamb add 3 ounces of salt, 1 tablespoonful of sweet sauce, 1 tablespoonful of Fun Wine, and a few threads of orange skin. Mix well.

(c) By means of a funnel fill this mixture into the lining. Put a knob about every six inches. Punch plenty of small holes with a needle.

(d) Expose in the hot sun for 1 day. Put in a windy place for 4 days. The air should be dry, so it is best to make these in the fall or winter. Never make them in the summer or spring.

Put the frankfurters in a china jar for at least 5 days before using them — the longer, the better.

Steam for ½ hour before serving. Serve with fried potatoes or fried gray potatoes underneath.

Gold and Silver Frankfurters

GOM NUN CHUNG

(a) Get the outside lining of the small intestine of a pig. Wash thoroughly with salt and then put into hot water for 10 minutes. Tie one end, force air through from the other end, and tie. Dry in the hot sun.

(b) Cut pork into pieces ¾ inch by ¾ inch by ¾ inch. To every pound of pork add an equal amount of pig liver, which has been rubbed with salt, washed thoroughly, and cut into pieces the same size as the pork. To this add 3 ounces of salt, 1 tablespoonful of Fun Wine, and a few threads of orange skin. Mix well.

(c) By means of a funnel fill this into the lining. Put a knob about every six inches. Punch plenty of small holes with a needle, to let in the air.

(d) Expose in the hot sun for 1 day. Put in a windy place for 4 days.

Keep them in a china jar for at least 5 days before serving.

Steam in a double-boiler for ½ hour. Serve with fried potatoes or fried gray potatoes underneath.

Spiced Pork

JUNG YORK

To each pound of pork use 2 ounces of spicery salt, 1½ teaspoonfuls of salt, 1½ teaspoonfuls of sugar. Mix and rub over the pork. Expose to the hot sun for 1 day. Dip into 5 ounces of sauce residue. Mash. Add 1½ ounces of sweet sauce, 2 ounces of good Fun Wine. Mix well.

Wrap up with Chinese tissue-paper, and put in a dry place where it can stay until dry. It is now ready for cooking.

(a) Cut 1 pound of spiced pork into pieces 1 inch by 1 inch by 1½ inches.

(b) Use about 10 bean cakes. Cut each cake into 4 pieces. Fry until yellow.

(c) Cut about 3 pounds of any Chinese vegetables into pieces the same size as the pork.

(d) Cook the pork, bean cakes, and vegetables in water in an oiled pan for ½ hour.

(e) Add Chinese gravy.

Dry Pork

LAB YORK

To each pound of pork use 3 ounces of salt. Rub all over and let stand for 1 night. The next morning wash the pork in hot water. Dry in the sun for 1 day.

When dry, rub well with a brush on which is sweet sauce and *Gong Chung,* Keep on doing this four times a day for 5 days.

Keep in a china jar one week before cooking.

Gong Chung is a residue of another kind of Chinese sauce.

Spiced Pork with Gray Potatoes

WO TOU JING JUNG YORK

1 pound spiced pork
2 cups gray potatoes
A few Chinese onions

(a) Cut the pork and the potatoes into pieces 1 inch by 1 inch by 1½ inches.

(b) Cook the pork, the potatoes and the onions in plain water in an oiled pan for ½ hour.

(c) Add Chinese gravy.

Dry Pork on Rice

LAB YORK FON

3 cups rice
1 pound dry pork

(a) Wash the rice 3 times. Put in a covered pan with 7 cups of water and cook until done.
(b) Place the pork on top of the rice. When dry remove to the back of the stove. Shake the pan frequently to prevent burning. Remove from the stove and keep the cover on for 10 minutes.
(c) Take out the pork and cut into the required size.
(d) Add salt and mix well.

Dry Pork with Gray Potatoes

WO TOU GE LAB YORK

To each pound of pork use 2 ounces of spicery salt, 1½ teaspoonfuls of salt, 1½ teaspoonfuls of sugar. Mix and rub over the pork. Expose to the hot sun for 1 day. Dip into 5 ounces of sauce residue. Mash. Add 1½ ounces of sweet sauce, 2 ounces of good Fun Wine. Mix well.

Wrap up with Chinese tissue-paper, and put in a dry place where it can stay until dry. It is now ready for cooking.

(a) Cut 1 pound of dry pork into pieces 1 inch by 1 inch by 1½ inches.
(b) Use about 2 pounds of bean cakes. Cut each cake into 4 pieces. Fry until yellow.
(c) Cut about 3 pounds of gray potatoes into pieces the same size as the pork.
(d) Cook the pork, bean cakes, and gray potatoes in plain water in an oiled pan for ½ hour.

Dried Pork with Fried Bean Cake and Chinese Vegetables

DO FO CHOY GE LAB YORK

(a) Cut 1 pound pork into pieces 1 inch by 1 inch by 1½ inches.
(b) Use about 10 bean cakes. Cut each bean cake into 4 pieces. Fry until yellow.

(c) Cut about 3 pounds of any Chinese vegetables into pieces the same size as the pork.

(d) Cook the pork, bean cakes, and vegetables in plain water in an oiled pan for ½ hour.

(e) Add Chinese gravy.

Dry Duck

LAB ARP

Duck can be dried successfully only in a certain place where the air is suitable; therefore the method need not be discussed here.

The best quality comes from Nan On, Kong Shi province, China. Next to that the best comes from Nan Hong, and from Kong Yon, Onong Duy province.

Dry Duck on Rice

LAB ARB BO FON

(a) Wash thoroughly 3 cups rice. Put it in a covered pan, add 7 cups of water, and boil until the rice is done.

(b) Put dry duck on top of the rice and cook until the water has evaporated. Shake the pan frequently to prevent burning. Remove from the stove and keep the cover on for 10 minutes.

(c) Take out the duck and cut into the required size.

(d) Add salt. Mix well.

Dry Flat Fish Chop Suey

CHOW YOU YUE

The best quality of dry flat fish comes from Kowlon, China. The poorest ones are those from Japan. They are thicker.

(a) Soak the dry flat fish for ½ hour. Wash thoroughly. Take off a piece of bone on the center of one side of it. On the bone side put knife-marks one-half as deep as it is thick, as shown in the figure. Then cut into 2 inches by 1½ inches.

(b) Put into the cut flat fish ½ teaspoonful of ginger juice, 1 tablespoonful of Fun Wine, 1 teaspoonful of crab juice.

(c) Soak 2 cups of dry mushrooms for ½ hour.

(d) Cut 1 cup of celery, 1 pound of any vegetable, a few pieces of pork, and a Chinese onion into pieces 1½ inches long.

(e) Cook the mushrooms, celery, vegetables, and pork in an oiled pan with primary soup until done.

(f) Put the fish into a very hot, oiled pan. Keep turning until it is rolled up like a piece of cigarette. Add the other ingredients and mix well.

(g) Add Chinese gravy.

Dry Flat Fish Soup

YOUT YUE TONG

1 pound dry flat fish
½ teaspoonful alkaline solution
12 cups primary soup

(a) Cover the dry flat fish with cold water. Add the alkaline solution. (Get this from a Chinese grocery store.) Soak for 15 minutes. Wash thoroughly, take out the bones.

(b) Cook the fish in plain water for 3 hours. Change the water several times while cooking. Then cook for 15 minutes in the primary soup.

Serve with the soup. Put into it a few drops of sesamum-seed oil.

Roast Dry Flat Fish

SUE YOU YUE

1½ pounds dry flat fish
1 tablespoonful peanut oil
1 cup red vinegar
A few drops sesamum-seed oil

(a) Wash the dry flat fish thoroughly. Rub over it a coating of oil or lard. Place on top of a charcoal fire by means of a wire. It is done when there are bubbles on the surface. Turn over and continue the same. Be careful not to let it get burnt.

(b) Tear the fish into threads. Mix with these threads the sesamum-seed oil, peanut oil, and red vinegar. Sugar to suit the taste.

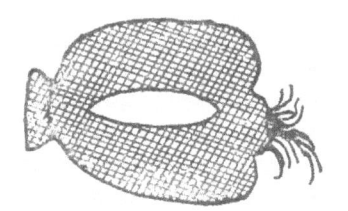

How to put knife marks on bone side of dry flat fish

Stove Party

DAK BIN LO

In cool winter evenings this party is very often found in the Chinese houses.

Put a small stove in the center of the table. On top of it place a pan of boiling primary soup. Cut into thin pieces 6 pounds of any food at all — such as pike, chicken meat, shrimp, beef, flat fish, etc. This food is uncooked.

Place one piece of it in the boiling primary soup for 2 minutes, using a fork or a chopstick to pick it up with. Keep moving.

Now put it into a bowl containing 1 well-beaten egg, 1 tablespoonful of Chinese sauce, ½ teaspoonful of oil, and a few drops of sesamum-seed oil. It is now ready to eat. One bowl of this egg should be served to each person.

Two forks or two pairs of chop-sticks are required for each person, one used for putting the meat into the pan, the other for eating.

Rice

BO FON

To 1 cup of rice use 2½ cups of water.

Cook in a covered pan, over a hot fire, until the water has evaporated. Remove to the back of the stove for a few minutes. Then take from the stove and keep the pan covered for 10 minutes.

The flavor of the rice is greatly improved by adding butter and salt.

Fried Rice

CHOW LON TON

4 bowls cooked rice
¾ pounds chicken or pork cut into cubes
2 cups secondary vegetables
5 eggs
1 cup primary soup

(a) Put the rice in a hot, oiled pan and cook until it changes color, turning frequently with a cooking-shovel.

(b) Fry the chicken and secondary vegetables for 3 minutes in a hot, oiled pan. Add cold water and cook for 15 minutes. Pour off the water and add the rice.

(c) Beat the eggs well and add to the rice.

(d) Add the primary soup and continue to cook until the egg appears to be done.

Chinese Meat Biscuit

SANG YORK BOW

6 cups flour
1 yeast cake
2 small tablespoonfuls salt
1 tablespoonful sugar
3 potatoes
1 tablespoonful lard

(a) Wash and pare the potatoes. Cover with cold water. Boil until tender. Mash the potatoes in the same water in which they are boiled. Let stand until just luke-warm.

(b) Put in the salt and sugar.

(c) Add the lard and yeast cake. Dissolve thoroughly.

(d) Sift the flour thoroughly and put into a pan. Make a hole in the middle of it. Slowly pour in the potato mixture. Mix well.

(e) Dredge the hands well with flour. Turn the dough out on the mixing-board. Use as little flour as possible on the hands when kneading the dough — only enough to keep the dough from sticking to the hands. Knead for 10 minutes.

(f) Put into a pan. Cover well with a towel and let stand overnight.

(g) In the morning turn out on the mixing board. Divide in half, as this quantity makes 2 nice loaves of bread. Now knead each loaf separately. Let stand until it rises to double the size.

(h) Cut into the size of biscuits, and roll flat.

(i) Add chopped roast pork, chopped frankfurter, red cheese, and salt, and wrap up into a ball. Close it carefully, making a perfect ball of it. The amount of meat and cheese should be about one-half that of the dough.

(j) Place in a double-boiler for 10 minutes before putting on the stove. Steam for ¾ hour.

Cake

Almond Cake

HON YUN BUEN

1 pound flour
½ pound sugar
½ pound lard
5 eggs
¼ teaspoonful alkaline solution

(a) Mix the flour, sugar, lard, eggs, and solution well on a suitable board. Add a little quantity of lard at a time until every particle of flour will contain an equal amount of each substance.

(b) Make into a cake of any desired size. In the center of each place an almond.

(c) Put into a suitable pan and bake in the oven until nicely browned. The length of time depends on the temperature of the oven and the amount of cake.

Chinese Sponge Cake

GUY DON GO

10 eggs
1 pound sugar
2/3 pound flour
A few drops of lemon juice

(a) Beat the eggs in a suitable bowl. Mix well with sugar. Beat for an hour, being careful always to beat in one direction.

(b) Mix with the flour and lemon juice.

(c) Put into a suitable pan and steam for ¾ hour.

Pudding

Water Chestnut Pudding

MAR TI GO

2 cups water chestnut powder
1 cup sugar
6 cups water

(a) Dissolve the water chestnut powder in a little cold water. Mash well.
(b) Now add the sugar and the 6 cups of water. Stir well.
(c) Put into a suitable pan. Steam until done (about 1 hour).

Lily-Root Pudding

OUT FUN GO

2 cups lily-root powder
1 cup sugar
6 cups water

(a) Dissolve the lily-root powder in a small quantity of cold water. Mash well.
(b) To this add the 6 cups of water and the sugar. Stir well.
(c) Put into a suitable pan. Steam until done (about 1 hour).

Gray Potato Pudding

WO TOU GO

1 cup dry pork
1 cup dry shrimp
1 cup dry Chinese olives
1 cup dry Chinese frankfurters
1 cup dry Chinese onions
2 pounds gray potatoes
1 pound Chinese gim-flower

(a) Cut into small pieces the pork, shrimp, olives, frankfurters, and onions.

(b) Pare the potatoes. Rub them on a rough grater, or on a board having plenty of nails pointing out 1/16 inch.

(c) Mix all of the ingredients together with 2 bowls of plain cold water. Salt to suit the taste.

(d) Put into a suitable pan and steam for 1 hour.

Candy

Peanut Candy

FAR SUNG TONG

1 pound peanuts
½ pound sugar

(a) Fry the nuts in a hot pan for 10 minutes. Take off the skins.

(b) Put 1 bowl of water in a hot, oiled pan. To this add the sugar. Cook, stirring constantly, until there is no water left.

(c) Mix the peanuts with the sugar on a board. Roll while hot until the mixture is ½ inch thick. Let cool.

(d) Cut to desired size.

Sesamum-Seed Candy

GE MAR TONG

1 pound sugar
4 ounces cornstarch
2 handfuls sesamum-seeds

(a) Oil pan well. Pour into it 1 bowl of water and then the sugar and cornstarch. Cook until no water is left.

(b) Roll out on a board sprinkled with the sesamum-seeds. Roll into balls or bars. Let cool.

Conclusion

The Chemistry of Foods

The most important thing is that food should be of the proper quality. Quality is more important than quantity. Food must also be of the right kind and in season.

A cook should know what the different foods contain, so that he can pick out the most nutritious.

Fat only is not a benefit to the body, but when combined with other foods it is used as fuel.

The value of food as a source of energy is stated by a heat unit called a calory. A calory is the amount of heat required to raise the temperature of one kilogram of water one degree centigrade. The fuel value of foods may be computed in a different manner.

Different foods require different lengths of time for digestion.

The following table gives approximately the time it takes each substance to be digested and the number of calories developed per ounce.

Foods have two purposes: first, the repair of muscular waste; second, the supply of the body with fuel to keep its heat at about 98°. Both are necessary to life.

Food	Number of ounces per 100 calories	Number of hours for digestion
Almonds	160	2½
Bamboo shoot	137	3
Barley		2¼
Beans	2.66	2
Bean Cake	192	3
Beef	1.4	4
Celery	5.3	3½
Chestnuts	70.3	3
Chestnuts (dried)	30	3½
Chicken	3.24	2½
Cornstarch		3
Dates	101	2
Duck	65.6	4½
Eggs	2.1	2 to 3½
Fish	4.85	3
Fowl	65.6	3
Chinese Ham	1.21	4 to 5
Lamb	51.2	2½ to 3½
Lettuce	15.2	2¾
Lobster	4.13	4
Melon, East	25.7	1¾
Melon, Star	18	1½
Muskmelon	11.6	1½
Mushrooms	13.1	1½
Mushrooms (dried)	2.4	2¾
Nuts	189.4	2 to 3
Oysters	6.82	2¼
Oysters (dried)	1.9	3¾
Peanuts	.52	3
Potatoes	24.1	2¼
Potatoes (gray)	27.6	3½
Pepper		2½
Quail	48.4	
Rice	3.1	3
Sugar	.86	
Tomato (Chinese)	3.24	2¾
Turkey	85	3 to 4
Walnuts	189.4	3½
Water Chestnuts	97.6	2¾
Watermelon	.27	1

Nitrogen is the muscle making substance. It is an important ingredient of albumin, which is found in its most perfect form in the white of an egg. Ham, beef, venison, chicken, and beans also are rich in nitrogen.

The carbon needed to keep up the body's heat is found in rice, cornstarch, potatoes, beans and oil.

Onion also is valuable as a food.

Too much fat is not healthful for the body.

Man under varying conditions spends different numbers of calories of heat. The following table gives approximately the hourly expenditure of energy of the normal person when asleep, awake, at work, and at rest.

Condition of muscular Activity	Average calories per hour
When sleeping	65 calories
When sitting up	100 "
In light exercise	170 "
In moderately active muscular exercise	290 "
In severe active muscular exercise	450 "
In very severe active muscular exercise	650 "

Now, having considered the kinds of food necessary for health, let us see why Chinese food is better than ordinary food.

Meats contain too much nitrogen in proportion to other substances. Vegetables contain everything necessary to sustain life. But a pure vegetable diet has much waste material, such as the cellulose forming the walls of the plant-cells, which is indigestible. Hence when the two are combined in the right proportion the diet is the best possible for man.

Chinese food furnishes just this mixed diet.

When a man sees or smells something that is tasty his mouth begins to water. The water is a dilution of hydrochloric acid, with which food is digested. If he does not chew his food long enough to let the water form and mix with the food, he has a sickness known as indigestion. When he goes to a physician the physician will give him some form of dilute hydrochloric acid to digest his undigested food, and so he will feel all right. Since Chinese food is prepared in so tasty as well as fancy a way, it makes one's mouth water the moment you look at it. Therefore it makes indigestion impossible.

NAMES OF STORES AND NOODLE SHOPS WHERE CHINESE GROCERIES MAY BE SECURED

Hip Chung Wing
Chinese Chop Suey Supply
11 Mott Street
New York City

Tuck High Company
Chinese Grocery Store
19 Mott Street
New York City

Quong Yee Sing Company
Chinese Grocery Store
32 Mott Street
New York City

Tai Jan & Company
Chop Suey Supply
45 Mott Street
New York City

Quong Tuck Wing Company
Chop Suey Supply
59 Mott Street
New York City

Yat Kan Min Company
Noodle Shop
192 Park Row
New York City

LIST OF ARTICLES WITH APPROXIMATE PRICES
AND CHINESE SIGNS

Articles	Chinese Signs	Price	Per
Alkaline Solution	梘水	$ .05	small bottle
Almonds, Salted	醃炒杏仁	.75	pound
Bean Cake	豆付磚	.025	piece
Bean Sprout	牙菜	.15	pound
Bean Stick	付竹	.24	pound
Beans, Red	赤小豆	.12	pound
Beans, White	白豆	.08	pound
Bird Nest	燕窩	2.50	pound
*Bug Kay	北其	.10	handful
Calcium Powder	石膏	.10	tablespoonful
Cheese, Red	南乳	.25	jar
Cheese, White	付乳	.24	jar
Chestnuts, Water	馬太	.25	pound
Chow Chow	瓜英	.23	jar
Chow Min	炒面	.10	pound
Dates, Red	紅棗	.01	piece
Dong Chong Chow	冬虫草	.25	small bundle
Dong Sum	党參	.10	handful
Flour, Chinese	占米粉	.25	pound
Frankfurters	臘腸	.55	pound

* Bug Kay is a plant used for nourishment.

Fungus	云耳	$ .10	handful
Fun Wine	汾酒	.05	handful
Garlic, Dry	蒜頭干	.10	teaspoonful
Gay Zee	杞子	.01	piece
Ginger	生薑	.15	jar
Ginger, Sour	酸薑	.20	jar
Gong Chung	干醬	.50	pound
Ham, Chinese	火腿	.10	handful
Lily-Flower, Dry	金針	.25	pound
Lily-root Powder	藕粉	.10	pound
Melon, East	東瓜	.15	pound
Melon, Star	絲瓜	.88	pound
Mushrooms	毛菇	1.40	pound
Mushrooms, Dry	冬菇	.13	pound
Noodles	麵	.50	pound
Nuts, Lotus	蓮子	.35	pound
Nuts, White	白果	.10	handful
Octogon Spicery	八角	.40	pound
Olives, Chinese	杬角	.05	small bundle
Onions, Chinese	生蔥	.75	pound
Oysters, Dry	毛支	.23	pound
Peanut Oil	生油	.16	can
Pineapple, Canned	矸頭波羅	.16	pound
Potatoes, Gray	芋頭	.15	pound
Rice	白米	1.25	bottle
Sauce, Chinese (See Yout)	豉油	$ .40	bottle
Sauce Residue, Chinese	原豉	.15	jar
Sauce, Sweet (Cheu-You)	珠油	.36	bottle
Sesamum-seed	芝蔴	1.25	pound
Sesamum-seed Oil	蔴油	.44	bottle
Shark Fins	魚翅	2.60	pound
Shrimp, Dry	蝦米	.50	pound
Spicery Powder	香料粉	.10	spoonful
Tomato, Chinese	矮瓜	.15	pound
Vermicelli, Chinese	粉絲	.18	pound
Vinegar, Red	浙醋	.35	bottle
Walnuts	合桃	.25	pound
Why Shon	淮山	.10	handful
Cooking-shovel	鑊剗	.35	piece
Double-boiler	蒸籠	3.00	set
Frying-pan	鐵鑊	2.50	piece
Ladle	鐵殼	.25	piece